BARN
DANCE

Other books by the author

Stable Relation

Relaxed & Forward

Anna Blake

BARN DANCE

Nickers, brays, bleats, howls,
and quacks: Tales from the herd.

Cover design and formatting by JD Smith

Published by Prairie Moon Press
All enquiries to annamarieblake@gmail.com

First published 2016

To my family such as they are:

Before Noah's Ark and across time,
some of our relations were always meant
to have fur and feathers and scales.
I think that was always the plan.

HORSE/HUMAN CREATION STORY

In the beginning, humans ate horses. Some Neanderthals still do. About 25,000 years passed and one day a human—I personally think it was a woman—heard a voice in her head that she didn't recognize. It was a deep soft voice, like Barry White, only 5,956 years too soon. The human looked for the cause of the voice and saw a horse—I personally think it was a white horse. The human was a bit unsettled, so the horse took a deep breath and exhaled, and sure enough, the human mimicked him.

The horse thought there might be a chance that this frail human had a soul, so he offered his help.

And that's how humans domesticated the horse.

WHAT OTHER WOMEN DO ON SATURDAYS

It was years ago now. A riding friend and I had been invited to an art showing in the home of a mutual friend. The hostess had a lovely home with lots of charming detail and my friend was particularly enthralled by some dainty cheese servers with ceramic floral handles. Where did the hostess find these curious little things?

I informed my friend, with a sophisticated, worldly, and slightly sarcastic tone, that other women shop on Saturdays. They call a friend, go to lunch, and then shop for these sorts of things. It's what they do instead of going to the barn. She rolled her eyes but we decided to give it a try.

We picked a rainy day and let the barn rest. We had a leisurely lunch of salads and white wine, in clothes that were still clean by noon. We went to Printemps, a French department store that was in Denver at that time. Its displays were works of art, each and every one. It was the kind of store that can transport you to a different world for a while.

So, we gasped at Hermes scarves with familiar equestrian images. We fingered cashmere sweaters and flimsy under-things that wouldn't survive one ride. We finally landed in the shoe department where I tried on some delicate sky-blue suede pumps with squatty heels. They were ethereal, like walking on clouds. As I admired my feet in the mirror, I remarked to my friend, "Not great barn shoes…."

The saleswoman was very professional, impeccably made up, and expensively dressed. She turned to me and with a British accent, asked, "Oh, do you keep horses?"

I knew her question was meant to be light and conversational, but it struck me funny because she was so right. I had to answer in the most literal way. With a big smile, "Yes, I keep them. That is what I do, I buy them as babies or rescue them and I keep them till they're ancient. I never sell them, I keep them." My friend gave a snort.

I'm not sure why I remember this interchange so vividly all these years later. It was a small moment. My friend and I finished our day of shopping. We were back at the barn the next Saturday and have spent hundreds of happy weekends there since. Printemps eventually closed its doors. Still no cheese knick-knacks but our homes are decorated with photos of past equine companions and we're generally pleased if we don't have too many bits and stray gloves lying on the kitchen counter.

I still have the horse I was riding at the time of our shopping excursion. Spirit is retired now, with worn-out legs and crippling arthritis. Our list of past accomplishments is long and he's a faithful friend. The sort of horse whose heart had always been so big that anything was possible. Not one penny was squandered, not one Saturday was wasted. Spirit doesn't turn heads now; he looks like any other old horse—except to me.

Eventually, I bought a small property where he could retire in peace. Our best years are probably behind us, this old campaigner and me. And lots of difficult choices are ahead. For now, he shares his barn with a family of horses, donkeys, and the occasional goat, all secure in their future. Sometimes at the dawn, if you squint just right, the light turns this old white horse pink.

As for those silly frail shoes that I tried on that day, I didn't buy them, in favor of the less stylish steel ones that my horse wears. When I think back to that Saturday spent doing what other women do, I have no regrets. I'm a wildly lucky woman. I keep horses.

THE BARN RAT RELEASE

First, let's get our terminology straight. A barn rat is a child who might answer a thumb-tacked ad at the feed store with the headline *Horse-Crazy Girls Wanted*. (Yes, almost always a girl.)

The Infinity Farm barn rat is nine years old. Elana got here the usual way, begging and badgering parents who don't ride. Through extended connections, she showed up one day for a lesson on Max, to be paid for with her birthday money. The thank-you note she sent had all of us in tears, and the rest is history.

Sometimes the barn rat arrives to the news that she can't ride that day. Elana is just as cheerful about mucking as riding. She weighs a fraction of a full muck cart and grunts like a linebacker when lifting a shovel of manure. She's working off part of her lesson and if it's horse related, it's important.

Sometimes she helps me doctor a wound, applying the ointment with small gentle fingers. Sometimes she holds horses for the farrier, examining hoof trimmings and old shoes. Last visit, Max got a bath that cooled all of us off. If you ask her to fetch something and there's a horse between her and the object, know that it will take her a while to get it done.

When it's time to tack up, Elana's grooming process begins with a step I didn't teach her. She stands at Max's shoulder and places both hands, palms flat, on his shoulder and flank. She moves her hands in small circles, swaying silently. I timed this part during her last visit. After twelve minutes, I quietly

4

suggested it might be time to start with the currycomb.

Finally, time to ride; she speaks firmly, loves a trot, and does her very best. I teach her that when her horse is good, she should reward him with a release; a kind word or a scratch on the withers. She does fail at that. Her release is nothing short of a full body hug on his neck. But the old horse whisperers say that the release should be bigger than the ask, so that's fine with me.

We are a barn of mainly adult riders. I notice that the quality of the lessons I give always goes up after a barn rat visit. Thanks for the reminder, Elana.

THE PERFECT PURSE

That's what I called my first truck—the perfect purse. It could carry all I needed for work and barn, and if folks didn't want to be up front with me and the dogs, they could ride in the shell on back—along with assorted saddles and art supplies, boots and feed. The dogs were here first, after all.

My trucks have always been pre-owned and more practical than pretty. My current truck is scratched and dented, and missing the jump seat in its extended cab. Or maybe it came "customized" without one for more room for dogs and dog beds. I lost the tailgate dragging nine-hundred-pound hay bales out using tie straps. Sometimes I intentionally use my ball hitch as a weapon and other times it's just an accident.

This particular truck was my first lemon. I had so many repairs on it the first year that friends bought me a set of tires out of pity—it was that bad. We persevere, like you might with a stray dog that never quite joins up but doesn't actually leave either.

Sometimes when I'm in town, I see men driving fancy trucks with lots of chrome and spotless bed liners. I wonder if that truck ever gets to do an honest day's work. Maybe those men only drive them to the strip mall to get their nails done. I bet that truck looks at our load of demolished fencing and corrugated tin with envy. Does washing and polishing embarrass a truck—like a tomboy forced to wear a Sunday dress?

This week my truck let loose a serious stink and complained

mightily while pulling a trailer with three horses up a steep hill. I'm waiting for the call from the repair shop now. I do love the right tool for the job; a truck whose tire treads are thinner in back from pulling, and side panels with equidistant scratches as far apart the teeth on a T-post. There is beauty in strength, but I'm not sentimental about machines.

In the end, I would hate my truck to be mistaken for my primary form of transportation. That position will always be held by a handsome, well-groomed horse, with more tune-ups than my truck and more hair product than me.

HAMSTERS WILL NEVER REPLACE HORSES

Has it been one of those weeks? When everything that could go wrong did? We all know how it feels when gravity gets extra heavy-handed and you begin to feel thick and bound by life. It happens. Maybe you should go to the barn and let yourself be carried for a while.

If you have a partnership with a horse, then you know that some days you carry them and some days they carry you. You *carry* them by caring for them and keeping them safe and warm. If there is an injury, you help it heal. When the training is hard, you reward them generously. When the going is slow, you give them patient encouragement. It's being somewhere between a parent and a friend, only better.

Some days they *carry* you. On the days when gravity is too constricting, you can climb up top. It can be as simple as getting your lead feet off the ground. The quality of air is sweeter and cooler from the back of a horse. As the rhythm of your horse's stride loosens your body, your breath goes deeper and it's easier to remember everything will be all right. Again, somewhere between a parent and a friend, only better.

There is no loss of honor; no embarrassment in asking for help. Horses and their people learn to depend on each other, knowing that the favor will be returned again when needed. Sharing trust with a horse is a living sanctuary, a safe place from the inclement elements.

One of the things I appreciate most about working with clients and their horses is watching this trust grow as it is passed back and forth. Sometimes lessons start with a very distracted rider, and sometimes it's the horse who can't focus. Either way, a shift begins with the first few strides. Moving forward means not staying stuck.

Then the rhythm of the ride takes over like a moving meditation and soon resistance on both halves fall away. Together the horse/rider grow larger, stronger, and more beautiful than the sum of their parts. Even gravity is intimidated by that!

"In my opinion, a horse is the animal to have. Eleven-hundred pounds of raw muscle, power, grace, and sweat between your legs—it's something you just can't get from a pet hamster."
—Author Unknown

I'm willing to give equal time to hamster owners. Anybody?

IT'S MORE THAN THE HAT

Willard Boone was the first man I fell in love with. I was five when we met and he was certainly in his thirties. It didn't feel like a February-September sort of romance to me though. He wore jeans and a white pearl snap shirt, top collar button fastened. And a cowboy hat, of course. We were in farm country and ball caps were the norm. Cowboy hats were just on TV shows like *Bonanza*. Maybe Willard was actually Ben Cartwright's long lost son?

My grandfather was a horse dealer and Willard Boone did business with him. Our farm was a day's haul east of there on the state highway, so Willard would drive up our driveway once a year or so, lay up overnight or stay for a meal, and then be off again. The only thing I knew about him was what the men said: Willard would pick up "bad" horses that no one else wanted but somehow, if you ever got the chance, it was a smart thing to buy a horse from him. Willard was kind of a legend, but he seemed to make folks a little uncomfortable, too.

The men on our farm were loud but Willard had a quiet voice, low and deep. Incredibly, he'd push his hat back and squat down to look me in the eye. He paid attention to my little girl questions and spoke to me as if what I had to say mattered. It wasn't done on our "seen and not heard" farm and I never forgot it.

Looking back, his almost mystical reputation makes me wonder if Willard was what some would call a horse whisperer.

Positive re-enforcement isn't a new method of training. Xenophon wrote about it in 400 BC; it's been around forever but it certainly wasn't the way things were done on our farm.

This year I met that kind of cowboy again. He wore a starched Wrangler shirt and creases in his jeans. When greeting me, he doffed his hat, made eye contact, and shook my hand firmly. We spent a day together at a film shoot where he was an expert and I was a demo rider. He generously shared his insight and knowledge with me, all the time complimenting the work my horse and I had done. My horse was totally taken with him, and I was, too.

And I was reminded of Willard for the first time in a while. These men were both cut of the same crisp cloth. Nothing has changed in the last fifty years. I may ride in an English saddle now, but I'm still grateful to Willard and cowboys like him who live by a code inspired by a higher vision. Kindness and respect is still the best approach with horses, and children, and truly, every other living thing.

BARN CATS

My best barn cat was Hank. He and his sister, Squirrel, were in a free-kittens box in the feed store parking lot. The price was right and they were dirt-gray tabbies. Brighter colors are hawk bait. I kept them inside till they were nine months old and neutered.

Then Hank went out to feed with me, and in the time it took to get grain out, he had a couple of tiny victims already laid out in the morning sun. Yes, in the spring he substituted baby bunnies, but I can't nitpick too much. Hank is a big guy and not satisfied with small vermin. He progressed to adult rabbits and eventually Hank got the taste for being a bully and started in with dogs. Size didn't matter; it was all good sport.

I was on the phone one Sunday morning, looking out the window when two coyotes turned up my driveway and headed for the house. One was Half-Tail, the big male that I knew from the pond. They usually don't travel down the middle of the road, much less turn up my drive. I chatted away as he and his mate got closer, and I got more interested. Half-Tail had made his way to my front steps. I was right in the front window, two feet away, and he didn't pause. He was on a mission. I peered out the window sideways to see what Half-Tail saw and there was Hank with a rabbit. Half-Tail, who wanted lunch the easy way, tried to take the rabbit from Hank, who was not in the mood to share. They were having a tug of war over this mostly dead rabbit and I didn't care to see how it turned out. If Hank managed to beat up a coyote we would never hear the end of it, and if Half-Tail mangled Hank, I didn't want to explain it to the vet. I threw the door open, loud and fast. Half-Tail took a big jerk and Hank was left, back arched and giving a deep scream that a mountain lion would have been proud of. Half-Tail left with the rabbit and Hank's pride.

Hank kept the vermin under control, and Squirrel took on moths and flies. Somehow, she left paw prints of moth dust on windows everywhere. I had hit the jackpot with these two hard-working cats.

They almost made up for Ivy. She was a rescue cat who was a two-year-old, long-haired tortoise-shell in good health, or so they said. They got the color right. When I arrived to meet her, she was matted and was missing at least half her teeth. Eight would have been an overly-flattering guess at her age. She had been de-clawed, which not only disqualified her as a barn cat, but means she was partly disabled. She'd been living in an old car for two years. I was sure she could do better with us.

It didn't take long to figure out why Ivy had been ostracized to the car. Her litter box requirements were a bit high, which she let me know by not using it. Once we got past that and her mats, Ivy settled in like an old dowager. She went outside twice a year, as far as the front porch where she napped on a lawn chair. Once she did walk to the side of the house and saw the horses. She was so appalled that she didn't come out again for a year. During the last year of her dotage, I found her with a dead mouse. There was some question; did she actually bite it to death with her one remaining canine tooth or maybe she sat on it until it expired? Either way, a job well done. She helped me in the kitchen, peeling shrimp and such. She still paid her way; sometimes it is enough to just not be Hank.

EDGAR RICE BURRO ON THANKS-GIVING

Slow down. No one's tombstone ever says "I wish I'd mucked faster."

Edgar Rice Burro has lots of opinion when I muck the pens. He runs to greet me, which usually results in him blocking the gate I'm trying to get through. That takes some un-tangling. Once I'm in, he carefully positions himself over the top of a muck pile, between me and the muck cart, in the perfect spot to make it impossible to actually get a fork-full to the cart. Then he refuses to move and all my shushing falls on long and deaf ears. So, I flail my arms and maybe even stomp my feet. Edgar doesn't budge. He's patient with lower life forms; he waits until I pull my rude and unfocused self together and put down my fork.

You might think he wants something but I never carry treats. This isn't about that. Edgar has something to give me but first he needs me to pay attention. He's elegant in his simplicity, eloquent without words; he just wants a still moment to let me know that he's grateful. Sometimes Edgar gives me a lean, sometimes a nuzzle. There's a shared breath that just takes a moment and I'm reminded that poop isn't the most important thing. For thanks-giving to work, there's some thanks-taking required on my part, as well. Then Edgar allows me to finish mucking his pen while lurking close at my heels. We move on together to the next pen; mucking is a chore to be savored for the company, if not the actual task.

Living in a herd where I'm the minority species is a constant education for me but I have to slow down to be a good student. Donkeys (or any other animal) aren't a career, or a hobby, or a passion. The investment in time and money is great, but they aren't a possession. First and foremost, they are each a life, whole and true. When we acknowledge that they exist not just in our shadow, but in full dimension, with conscious intelligence to share, a door opens that we miss if we limit animals by over-humanizing them. They live in a larger, natural world that expands past our individual human *hill-of-beans* lives. Respect for animals is an affirmation that each of us share part of a greater Life. Some part of Edgar knows that and it isn't just that they can't live without us. We can't do without them either. I'd bet my muck fork on it.

WHAT A PARROT TAUGHT ME ABOUT HORSES

There were a few dark years between leaving home and having enough income to support a horse, that I was earthbound with only house pets. I survived it. Barely.

During that horse-less time, a package arrived. It was a surprise *parrot* from a friend in Panama. I'm not saying it was a great idea to catch a bird and ship her, I'm just saying that she arrived.

The parrot looked pretty rough right out of the box. Her feathers were oily and fairly ratted-out. She was kind of a *mustang* of a parrot—disoriented and frightened. Returning her to the wild wasn't possible and we didn't like each other much. I named her Trixie, as an affirmation of better days ahead.

Before long Trixie was willing to take a snack from my fingers, getting squirt-bottle showers, and talking with the television. Her feathers were a sleek emerald green color with a bright yellow crown on her head. Neither of us wanted her caged forever so I let her out without having a plan of how to get her back in. Short-sighted, I admit. She tossed the kitchen, pooped on the art, and pierced the cat's ear. Twice. Then I watched her turn a set of wooden window shutters into matchsticks with her very impressive beak. Parrots might be the *Jaws of Death* of the bird world.

Most parrots are hand-tamed as babies before their *Jaws of*

Death are fully developed. And the fact that she shrieked and cackled in *my own voice* did un-nerve me a bit. But I am no frail flower myself. I had a strong, rural upbringing, after all.

When it was time to try to catch her, I had enough pride to not use a fish net. I had noticed that she used her *Jaws of Death* beak to test any possible perch, so I got some gloves and approached her. She cocked her head, looked me in the eye and checked the glove perch-ability. She judged it, with a glass-shattering scream, very bad. She seemed more frightened of the glove than she was of me. Message received.

So, I gave up on the glove and took one last look at my pasty-white index finger. I screwed up my courage and presented it to the parrot. She stretched her beak wide in a lip-licking sort of way and reached for my finger. I squealed, and jerked my finger back; she screamed in an obnoxious (yet familiar) voice. We startled each other when we were already scared.

It was a bad attempt, I didn't think it out, and hindsight was just as helpful as ever. Trixie flew away even more frantic—if that was even possible. Hours of domestic destruction followed as I slowly tried to get close again. Eventually she got hungry for actual food and we started over.

The next day I was able to offer my finger again, but with a little more commitment this time. Skeptical of my perch possibilities, Trixie was very cautious. This time when her beak stretched open again, I *stood in*. I held steady as she tested my finger's reliability again and again. I trusted her, not that I had any evidence that supported it, but one of us had to be the one to start.

It was a firm squeeze she gave me—sort of enthusiastically friendly, I tried to convince myself. Then she climbed on my finger and continued all the way to my shoulder. Trixie started a soft sing-song mumble as she sorted through my hair. The standoff was over and suddenly I was mimicking her as much as she was me.

I remember Trixie when I see a new rider—struggling to

find a veneer of confidence—pick up a hind hoof or prepare for a first trot. Even a seasoned rider can feel hesitation when trying something new. So, we *stand in* and let them know we are a reliable perch. Because to gain a horse's trust, we must first prove ourselves trust-worthy.

BOSS MARE: WOMEN AND HONESTY

Lately, I'm discovering I like mares more and more. They are so *not* like most of us humans. They have a refreshing honesty. "If you aren't going to drive the bus, get out of my way and I'll do it." Succinct, blunt, and clean with her intention—a mare will get the job done.

Thank you; it's a relief. Bluntness is a gift after so much of the usual passive-aggressive chatter. "Honey, would you mind, if you have a minute, and it isn't too much trouble...?" Why don't we just say what we mean already?

It's because many women were raised to think it's more important to be polite than honest; to put a smile on our faces, bite our tongues, and not make a scene. Many women perfect a passive-aggressive communication style that is indirect and manipulative, but on the surface, polite and caring. It's a communication style that can be funny in a sitcom, but it doesn't work with horses.

Horses are honest. The language of the herd is more of a "Say what you mean and mean what you say" approach. No one apologizes for their own feelings or tries to control outcome; they breathe and ask for what they want.

It's no surprise there's a natural clash of communication styles between horses and riders in the barn. A novice rider might give what she thinks is a clear cue and the horse ignores it completely. A smart mare may flick an ear, but then keep on "driving the bus" until someone qualified shows up to take over.

It's just common sense to ignore a nagging, whining passenger.

Eventually some of us will want a better relationship with our horses—or at least some steering—so riding lessons are an option. It's a little like couples' therapy. As a trainer, I don't usually see physically cruel riders in lessons; no one using whips and spurs in anger. But instead of asking for what we want clearly and then expecting an answer, we tease, cajole, nag, and in the worst cases, use the "if you really loved me..." threat to get our way with horses. Rather than introduce ourselves honestly, ask for what we want, and then say thank you, we try to trick them into a behavior. We stalk them like a coyote with ulterior motives.

Cathy Meyer, divorce coach, says "When someone hits you or yells at you, you know that you've been abused. It is obvious and easily identified. Covert abuse is subtle and veiled or disguised by actions that appear to be normal, at times loving and caring. The passive-aggressive person is a master at covert abuse."

Is abuse more acceptable in the guise of kindness? Does passive abuse destroy trust any less?

Horses are a bit ahead of humans in communication, or maybe just more straightforward. They avoid the emotional quicksand and proceed to the real issue. We should consider adopting their approach to make ourselves understood. Clarity and respect is the language of the herd and Boss Mare leadership is more about understated confidence and responsibility than popularity.

When horse-women spend enough time around Boss Mares, we eventually acquire this same brand of honesty with our own species as well. The more natural we become, the less we're welcome in ladies' parlors where gossip passes as truth and coyotes pose as royalty. We're less willing to use our skills of deception and more likely to just state the plain truth.

Have you crossed the Boss Mare line and become a social liability? Good for you.

A HARVEST MOON AND FALL FLU

The calendar changed and so did the weather. These first September days have been undeniably fall; shorter, crisper, with a bit more oxygen in the air. This weekend is the Harvest Moon, the full moon nearest the autumnal equinox. Our prairie will be illuminated, but I know what comes next. I won't say the word... but tick, tick, tick.

The horses didn't need a calendar to know. There's a barn-wide epidemic of the Fall Flu. Do you know the symptoms? Excessive bucking, farting and hair growth. There is no fighting this flu; best to give in and let it run its course. Literally. I peeled off the fly masks and fly sheets, and flung the pasture gate wide.

My filly got to the gate first, tail flagged and hooves churning up soil. She's blossomed this summer; her face is softer, she's more patient, and she moves with a new confidence. Our barn-baby-no-more, this harvest she is coming four, with a plan for world domination brewing.

The others follow her through the gate. Each horse is quirky, expressive, and dramatic in their bucking styles. Nubè gallops to the lead with his long strides but Grace is quick and agile. It takes all kinds to make a herd.

Last to the gate is my Grandfather Horse. His eyes are watery and his joints are somehow loose and stiff at the same time. He's eight years into a forced retirement and is still holding a grudge about it. But this summer he has softened some too. Maybe he's made peace with the passing time, probably more than I have.

As I pull his fly sheet, it's my bittersweet job to assess his chances for an easy winter. Weight's good enough but his legs are more unsteady. I know his vision is changing. The Grandfather Horse interrupts my worry to remind me that he isn't dead yet and this crisp season needs celebrating. As I release him, he lumbers to a trot with that familiar old flash to his tail. His arrival sends the herd into a fresh fit of bucking and farting.

From the gate, I ponder whether any of the other horses might need their feed adjusted in the coming months. Then there's that place in the fence needing repair while the ground is still soft enough to dig post holes. And I should test the water tank heaters and extension cords. The winter blankets will come down from the shelves. Summer droughts have pushed hay prices high already; I wonder if I can afford to buy extra hay ahead, just in case.

But right now, the pasture is alive with pounding hooves, a gang of gamboling llamas, and even a slow-loping donkey. It's the unfamiliar coolness after the thick heat all summer. And spring is frail and thin in comparison to the rich, textured maturity of fall. Harvest time indeed.

And the energy is contagious. I might be coming down with Fall Flu myself. No time to languish with thoughts of the cold months ahead. I'm in the middle of something here. My heels are twitchy, anxious to catch up with my herd.

CANADA GOOSE QUADRILLE

My corner of Colorado is having a particularly colorful autumn. The sun rise is later and later, but the dawn colors seem worth the wait. Tomatoes plants have wilted but the tree leaves are toasted to richness. I hear big weather is coming next week, so these are precious days.

Waterfront property isn't all that common in Colorado; my pond is one of a series of marshes, streams, and small reservoirs that wander across the prairie, guiding migrating birds. I used to be the sort of person who thought bird watching was for egg-heads. My pond has patiently taught me to sit down and shut up.

This week groups of Canada geese have been flying over—another sure sign of autumn. Some choose a lay-over on the pond, resting for a day or two on the way to warmer places. These bird-visitors might be my very favorite. You could question the morals of herons or great horned owls, but never Canada geese. They mate for life, and travel in a flock. (Horse-people call that a herd.)

Each time a flying "V" formation goes over, I pause and watch with respect. They have more quadrille experience than most of us. With each flap of the wing, *uplift* is created for the birds that follow. Research tells us that flying in this way, the flock has a 71 percent greater flying range than if each bird flew alone. They travel on the thrust of each other. (Sharing a common direction and working together makes the going quicker and easier.)

When the lead gander gets tired, he takes a break and falls to the back of the formation. Another will take his place and he can rest a bit as the formation continues on. (Many hands make light work.)

The geese in formation give a honk of encouragement to those flying ahead to keep up the good progress. Canadian geese are among the most talkative animals, with babies communicating to parents even before they are hatched. My pond is alive with their chattering! (Communication and encouragement enrich any experience.)

No bird is left behind: if a goose is sick or wounded, another pair of geese follow it to the ground and stay to protect it until it can fly again or it dies. Then they hitch a ride with another flock. (Living by the Golden Rule.)

Bird-watching ends up being comforting to me, especially on fall days when the news is sometimes sad. It's true that winter is on the way and ponds will freeze over. We might as well hibernate like depressed bears. The dark months go slowly for barn-dwellers braced from the cold.

Canada geese remind me there is comfort in numbers. Winter is quadrille season, horses and riders can fly in formation and share the warmth of a herd, the company of friends and cheers of support. You might need to be the lead goose for a bit, but it will be worth the effort later.

I SEE DEAD HORSES

It starts innocently. Maybe when you were little, your dad watched John Wayne movies like mine did. We fell in love with a column of cavalry horses (instead of their riders). We loved those horses until the cavalry met a band of Indians; Indian horses were always better. Or it may have been a horse movie like *My Friend Flicka* or *Black Beauty*, but we saw a tall horse on the screen, better than a gallant leading man, and a heart opened. The hook was set.

Years later while flipping channels, I came upon that cavalry column again, with the familiar soundtrack booming. (Growing up, I saw *She Wore a Yellow Ribbon* more often than I saw most of my relatives.) This time it occurred to me that those horses must all be gone by now.

I remembered my dear, crazy Uncle Gus who kept his draft team long after tractors made them obsolete. Our family considered the horses a useless folly, but when Gus hoisted me up onto the back of Big Bob, I understood why Gus couldn't say goodbye. Big Bob and Gus are decades gone now, but I know if Gus is driving something in the afterlife, it isn't his tractor. He would have understood about the movie horses.

There was a domino effect after that, realizing that all my childhood horse-friends were gone *as a whole*. It's simple math and obvious, for sure. Still realizing it gave me a feeling of quantum loss.

Yes, I see dead horses. My barn is haunted by movie horses

and childhood horse-friends. Then my post-childhood horse-friends. And okay, every horse I read about or that belonged to a someone I knew. And some I watched on YouTube. Probably even a few horses I passed in fields next to the freeway.

I love them, but horses are heart-breakers. Learning to live with loss is part of the agreement. If you are around horses long enough, you collect a fair-sized ghost herd.

I wouldn't change a thing. I like being reminded. It's a bitter-sweet taste lingering from the past. Missing them is sad, but to be honest, they each left me with a stronger, sweeter heart and it would be ungrateful to complain.

And it's no use trying to ignore them. Ghost horses are like grandparents off in the sitting room; companionably quiet family members, who linger past their years in memories as real as today.

For generations of horses: Big Bob and Lady, King and Cindy. For Touchdown and Rou, and especially Dodger—they're all welcome. I'm grateful for all those who brought me up and trained me. Feel free to haunt me anytime.

GRATITUDE FOR THE GIFT OF POOP

This is how you can tell there's a tourist in the barn: they keep their eyes on the ground and there's lots of erratic tiptoeing. Some even squeal at the sight of manure. I call it *Fecal*phobia—an irrational fear of digestive waste. Thankfully, humans are the only species prone to the disease. We're Nincom*poops*. Everybody else is fine about bowel relief.

People who live with horses don't get emotional about poop. It's such a normal part of the day-to-day reality; *Fecal*phobia is an urban luxury we just can't afford. More likely, horse owners appreciate a steamy monument affirming the health of their equine, remarking "Quelle Bon *Merde!*"

We wax poetic, *"A rose by any other name would smell as sweet."* —William Shakespeare.

But something happened this week that make me lose my sense of humor. During my late-night feed, I found my elderly gelding lethargic and wobbly. He'd had an explosive bout of diarrhea, his gut sounds were audible at a distance, and he actually burped loud and foul. (I know; horses aren't supposed to be able to burp.) My gelding collapsed to the ground and laid flat. He was in obvious pain but kind of listless at the same time. I feared the worst.

I finally got him to his feet an hour later, just as my vet arrived. We set to work in zero degree temperatures and howling winds to try to help my Grandfather Horse.

Diagnosis: Equine Colitis. How have I never heard of it? It's dangerous, like colic, with stress being a factor. Was this early, bitter winter weather the culprit? The treatment includes tubing fluids for dehydration and Banamine for pain, followed by Bio-sponge (a serious anti-diarrhea medication) and a course of pro-biotics.

My Grandfather Horse slowly got comfortable. My focused, hard-working vet eventually left, along with all my holiday money, in the wee hours. Farm calls like this confirm the total lack of romance in the veterinarian occupation, all the more reason I'm so grateful for someone to call.

I limped on frozen toes to the house to watch and wait. There's such a fine balance to an equine digestive tract. Once that process gets interrupted, there is no peaceful rest until that nutrition-elimination cycle is working normally again.

In pre-dawn light, I was thrilled to see the old gelding still on his feet. I continued his meds but he was still dull with no interest in hay. By mid-morning there was not much improvement; he'd chew a bit of hay but then spit it out. He seemed so depressed that I was at a loss. What else could I do? I brought him his best donkey-friend to share his hay snacks and remind him to swallow.

Each hour I cheerfully offered scraps of hay, each hour he would nibble. He took a bit of water. Excruciating hours crawled by. Then finally, just as the sun was setting, I saw it!

The incredible miracle of excrement!

*Turd*itis with projectile infermatude no more.

*Crap*tastic! *Fecal*icious joy! Fan*scat*ic release. Cow-pie-pretty *poop*itude!

*Stool*pendus healing!

*Turd*atious gratitude!

Hooray for poop. We all live to muck another day!

BEAUTY TIPS FROM THE BARN

I've been living and writing on this farm a few years now and I notice that no one is asking me for beauty tips. I wonder why not?

Sure, I call my truck the perfect purse but that's just common sense. It carries fencing tools, spare halters, and a few dogs. Otherwise known as farm cosmetics. If the place looks good, I look good, right?

Then there's my feet. If I can be permitted a vanity, it's my feet. I have straight toes that flow together to a gentle point, a long high arch, and slender, curved ankles. There's a beautiful thirty-year-old tattoo, a spray of iris flowers with long stalks that trace that subtle curve. Even if I keep all this beauty cleverly hidden in a pair of old muck boots with bulbous Minnie Mouse toes.

My hair has creative license, meaning flat spots of helmet hair, also known as *I-live-to-ride-another-day* hair. In the summer, I alternate that with garden hose hair.

I admit I don't dye my hair anymore. When I first moved to the farm, I tried to keep up the habit. I always did it first thing in the morning before I got distracted. I'd put the peroxide or dye on my hair and while waiting for rinse time, wander out to the barn to feed. Then I might tidy up the feed room or maybe fix some fence. Or just talk politics with the goats.

Awk! I'd lost time and the peroxide on my hair was dry, crunchy and way over-done. This can't be good. I raced to the shower, knowing that the water will rinse every hair off my head and leave a shiny, naked skull. But no, I did it several times, and amazingly, my hair was still attached. Eventually, even that got boring. Not to mention that a week or two after the dye job, my hair would turn a nasty rust color, from the ends moving up toward the skull. It might have been from the well water. It all started to feel too much like a science project so I quit the whole dye process. It goes without saying that I cut my own hair. I mean, as well as I can groom a horse, why not?

Then last month I was all set for a couple of spa days, complete with massage and hot soaks. Plans changed when my Grandfather Horse got sick and we had a costly midnight vet visit. I still took a couple of days, but not at the spa. I gave myself a facial; my skin can start to look a little like an old hay tarp from time to time. I used a product called Miracle Clay. It really is a miracle when ingested for equine ulcers and colic. (This clearly isn't a paid endorsement.) The package label says it's also a poultice, so I mixed some up with milk, lemon and honey and slathered it on my face. There was a big improvement; my skin had a smooth, girthed-up quality. I looked like a slightly younger fifty-seven-year-old woman who's out in the sun and wind every day.

And again, not that you asked, but here is my one real beauty tip and it works for everybody: Stand next to a horse you like. Or pull a couple of dogs on your lap. Then take a deep breath and feel your eyebrows soften. Let your eyes shine and feel the warmth of the inside of your smile.

Because natural cosmetics are the best.

JANUARY: THE MOURNING MONTH

Winter doldrums: I drag my feet all the way in from the arena. The ground is dry, the grass is dead, and the wind is a cold slap in the face. Maybe I have an *Auld Lang Syne* hangover. Mourning and a desire to hibernate go hand-in-hand in January. It seems we lose a lot of good people in this month. I'm missing a friend who passed six years ago this week.

We were an odd pair; Randi and I could not have been more different. Our best game over the years was trying on each other's shoes. Randi would have green, buttery-leather pumps—very Italian, and I would have woolly mukluks. She would have strappy stiletto sandals and me, red longhorn bull cowboy boots. We were both hopeless victims to our taste in shoes. We'd trade shoes, point at each other, and cackle like chickens. Try it; your shoes look silly on other people.

For all our differences, our lives mirrored each other. We lost our dads within weeks of each other and then four years later, both of our moms. Through twenty-five years of friendship, we celebrated art and dogs and living passionately.

I'm remembering a winter day when Randi brought her step-grand-daughter down to my barn for a long-promised ride. There was a sudden weather change. The wind was nasty, that January kind of cold. We couldn't talk the girl out of the ride, so we tacked up the Grandfather Horse. Once in the saddle, the girl's chin quivered uncontrollably. I've never seen a little girl so excited and miserable all at once. Randi and I pressed onto either side of my horse, squinting at each other over his mane. All four of us moved in a walking huddle, ducking our chins as we headed into the wind, shivering, and singing horse songs. Finally, we put up the gelding, gave him scratches and carrots, and headed in for hot chocolate. The perfect day.

I want to tell *all* the Randi stories, so you will miss her like I do.

A couple of years later there was similar weather for her graveside service, with snow on the trees and frost in my lungs. There was such an exquisitely painful moment as the casket was lowered. I felt the warmth of her friendship that day, too.

And now it's six Januaries later. I've lost more friends and horses and dogs since then. It's kind of warm, visiting with them in the winter. Winds blow, the earth is frozen and I still work to find a balance between hello and good bye. I notice that the older I get, the more practice I have.

"Excess of grief for the dead is madness; for it is an injury to the living, and the dead know it not." —Xenophon (RIP, 354 BC)

But there isn't much time to languish now. Days are longer already. Soon there will be mud, and even more horse hair on my clothes. The pond will thaw for baby ducks and miraculously, grass will grow. There are horses to start and people to meet. Hey, can I try on your shoes?

THE MARLBORO MAN ISN'T MY TYPE

The Marlboro Man isn't for me. He's the strong and silent type; it might be a romantic image on film, but it doesn't look like much fun in real life. He probably eats an unhealthy amount of meat; that's a given. A legendary smoker; no way would I let him in my barn. I doubt we would share the same taste in horses (or anything else.) A hug from the Marlboro Man would feel like carrying an arm load of sticks and cans—way too bony for my taste.

And wouldn't the Marlboro Man be looking at me squinty-eyed all the time? Nope, he's not for me.

Give me a Dude Rancher. Well, that's what he calls himself. He has a pair of Justin Ropers that he wore to our wedding. It's years later and they still look brand new. He has one of those flannel western shirts with an insulated lining. He calls it his house coat. The Dude Rancher drives a Subaru.

He saw a photo of me before we met and complimented my smile. It was a photo of me with a horse over my shoulder. I told him it was truth in advertising, there was *always* a horse over my shoulder. The Dude Rancher probably didn't believe me.

The first year he lived at Infinity Farm, I think he pretended that there were no buildings north of the house. You know what's on the north side, don't you? The Dude Rancher never had a dream to live with a crowd of animals in a *Little House on the Prairie*. His family thinks he's lost it. Still, he eventually became a member of our herd. The dogs are even starting to listen to him.

The Dude Rancher is handy with a hammer. He has built hay storage onto the barn and some great furniture. I'm glad he isn't wasting away, watching sports on TV while I'm in the barn.

He never offers to throw hay during blizzards but the Dude Rancher always asks if everybody is okay *out there*.

I don't mean to spark envy here, but the Dude Rancher does occasionally muck …on weekends …if it's warm outside …if there's not much going on …and it's too early for a nap. I notice that he does lose time scratching donkey ears and whispering to a certain bay mare.

Horses will never be a passion in the Dude Rancher's heart, but he shows the remarkable good sense to not be jealous of them. Men who complain about the amount of time or money women spend in the barn are just looking for trouble.

I know horse friends have who have found a positive version of a Marlboro Man, someone who shares horses and riding with them. Congratulations and much happiness.

Some of us prefer our men *not* in the barn too much. It's the Dude Rancher for me. If Geek Chic is the new cool, then he is at the very top of the list. Let your freak flag fly, Dude Rancher, glad to have you in the herd. Even if that means in the house.

The Dude Rancher and the Marlboro Man do have one thing in common: I wouldn't expect a grandiose gesture on Valentine's Day from either. They leave that to our horses.

COMPASSION FOR ALL
LIFE—NOT QUITE

This morning a lone Canada goose flew low over my pond, calling loudly, and looking left and right. She returned several times, searching back and forth overland between the small ponds most of the day. So clearly distraught, I wondered if she had lost her mate. Heart-felt goose sympathy...

If you've read my writing, I think it's pretty obvious how I feel about animals, and especially horses. To be clear I'm committed to any horse, any mustang, any donkey, any pony. And then, any age, any breed, any challenge. Of course, any place, any time. Finally, any equine not already mentioned.

If you are *un*familiar with my writing, I'll give you a synopsis. Horses are perfect. Donkeys are great thinkers. Generally, people are not a source of pride, unless they are working on being less of a problem for their horses.

I got my philosophy largely from Western movies in my formative years. I took the Native American side; not only did they have the best horses, but they didn't shoot buffalo from moving trains. There was a Great Spirit with a respectful circle of life philosophy; much more interesting to me than what the nuns were selling. If you tilted your head and squinted, there were no giant spiritual contradictions either.

But the devil is in the details.

My moral certitude about the value of life hits a bump with

flies. I don't like to kill them with chemicals; those same chemicals can be hard on horses. Instead, I buy fly predators and start a race war. That way I don't dirty my own hands with the killing. I sprinkle predators, while sweet talking the donkey, and leave the murder to nature.

I have bug hypocrisy. I feel so ashamed.

We are having a plague of miller moths currently. Looking toward the sunset from the tack room window, the view is nearly obscured by moths and their scat. Another million are flapping away, just out of frame. Can these zombie moths even have hearts?

This is my recurring nightmare: When I go out my front door and the tree explodes with a dense cloud of moths. If I don't control my breathing, all of a sudden I have a Patsy Cline hair-do with spit curls. I can hear a 1950's soundtrack—think Hitchcock. I am screaming, flailing my arms, and running for the town library. *The Moths!* A dark cloud chases me with a horrible dusty, moaning sound. Their moth excrement is leaving an obvious trail.

I confess—I'm teetering on the edge of Miller moth murder madness. It's them or me. Sometimes at night, when a few hundred moths are in my studio, I lose it. I grab my swatter and become Martina Navratilova, in her prime. I hit over-head smashes, whacking moths to the ground, furious and thrilled. Lampshades break, papers scatter, and dusty little carcasses land on my keyboard. The worst part is—I feel absolutely no remorse.

But after I catch my breath, I worry some radical, moth-loving arm of The People for the Ethical Treatment of Animals is plotting against me and my vigilante justice. Not to mention, every revenge-driven moth in a ten-state region. Paranoid? Not a bit. I stand firm, spit-curls adjusted, with swatter in hand!

EDGAR RICE BURRO, BON VIVANT

I think we all knew it was only a matter of time.

Edgar wanted me to wait to make this announcement, until after the award show season (Oscars, Golden Globes, etc.) He didn't want to steal the thunder from his friends. (Best Ass in a Supporting Role—it isn't one of the on-camera presentations.)

Newsflash: Our own Edgar Rice Burro is will be making his theatrical debut this spring. You could consider it off-off-off-Broadway.

We could not be more proud of him. And at the same time, you had to expect that it was going to happen. Donkeys like Edgar just naturally rise to the top. He's had a cult following for years.

As a public service, I have been asked to say a few words about Edgar, in an attempt to de-mystify his rather iconic persona and control the number of paparazzi helicopters flying over, waking up the goats at all hours.

Here goes: Handsome, most obviously, but beneath this athletic, viral surface there is so much more!

Naturally Edgar is a very interested in philosophy. It is not at all unusual to see him gazing with a Zen-like peace, thinking deep, soulful thoughts. He is very out-spoken verbally, holding forth with ageless donkey yodels—Edgar sings the blues. He prescribes to the time-honored hippie traditions of communal living and sharing your good fortune with friends.

He is very conservative in his personal habits, however. He

holds his hairs and doesn't begin to shed until after the very last freeze of late spring. He frequently worries that he might be over-dressed in his bay and white spots and would opt for a plain gray suit, if it were available. His nose is multi-lingual, including some dialects dating from prehistoric time.

Edgar likes children, cats, old horses, and pretty much anything that moves slowly. But he does find dogs a bit loud and abrasive. His favorite color is green—that spring color of green; grass green, alfalfa green, well, sweet-to-eat green.

Edgar has theatrical experience, of course. He and I did a bit of costumed performance art to Elvis's *Are You Lonesome Tonight?* It was Halloween and he wore a white crushed velvet cape with fringe. My cape was silver lame over crushed velvet bell-bottoms; we were worthy of Las Vegas. Then I sang out—loud and flat. (I think that's why he didn't sing along.) It was certainly the high point of my theatrical life.

Edgar's acting style is frequently compared to the easy grace of George Clooney. He's just that comfortable in his skin. Like many actors, Edgar is a bit shy in real life, humble about his leading-man good looks, and his Mensa membership. Edgar prefers speak for himself about his political opinions.

What is on the horizon for Edgar? I can't tell all, but Steven Spielberg has been on the phone with Edgar. He is filming a sequel to *WARHORSE*, about rebuilding people's lives after the war. Talks are going slowly; Streep is demanding Edgar, and she won't take no for an answer. Edgar refuses to fly and is concerned the availability of a good ear massage in England. Spielberg is willing to build the white cliffs of Dover and several other London sets, all in our south pasture, if Edgar will agree to star. Writers are scrambling to add a part for Fred, the duck. Negotiations continue.

PEACEDONKEY hopes to start filming this summer.

DO YOU THINK IT'S TIME TO CLEAN THE TRUCK?

My hay guy got a new truck. It's a pristine dually in a pearlized-platinum color with near Porsche-like lines. That big diesel engine hums like a finely-tuned tank. If there was a British Royalty truck edition, it would look like this. I liked it even more the second time I saw it, muddy and mussed. Should a dually really be this sexy?

I am the *other* kind of truck owner; I like my trucks broken in. By that I mean no worries about yet another dent, a hitch that I can use to demolish fence, and no pesky tail gate to get in the way.

My training business is mobile, so my truck doubles as a traveling tack room with whips on the dashboard and a tub behind the seat with various training gear. Then, all my tech lesson aids: a sound system, tablet computer, video camera. Depending on the day, I might have a wading pool in the bed. I keep ulcer and colic remedies handy. There are scattered notebooks with scribbled ideas and reminders, along with popcorn and ice tea. Living in Colorado requires at least three seasons of weather gear at all times. I like to keep a halter with me, in case I come upon any strays. And of course, at least one helmet. My truck is truly the perfect purse. There, I said it.

There is usually at least one wagging co-worker with me. My dogs see the truck as a kind of IMAX kennel and since I leave keys in the ignition, then the truck does need to be guarded. (Okay, no one else would *want* my truck, but still, a good dog like Howdy takes his job seriously.)

I have a kind of reverse pride in my truck; after all, a horse owner should never consider a truck their primary form of transportation. Would a stranger judge me harshly?

This week I was driving on a dirt road on the way to the next client appointment, and thinking about how great the last horse had done. Boom! Suddenly, a nose bleed—startling, colorful, dramatic! I never get nose bleeds! Awk!

I pulled over and stopped, tilting my head to the side, like that that would save me from a blood-splattered shirt. Now what? I never learned the tissue habit, just not in my upbringing. I look around the truck—nothing but a jacket. Howdy furrowed his brow. I never even open my glove box but I'm desperate, so I lean over and check it.

The latch opens to reveal tissue! Hooray, but it's totally shredded, or maybe exploded to fit the inside dimension of the box. It's a feather bed fluff of neat, clean confetti-sized pieces. Does somebody live here? I carefully pull some out for my nose, and then lean closer.

Stealth: I pull the top layer of tissue confetti aside to find another layer. It's like opening a present; Howdy leans in close. About three inches in, I find a tidy nest, woven from Howdy's long copper-colored hair at the center of the tissue shreds. Someone got loose dog hair from the seat and brought it here— so much work. Sweet and soft, this has been a little living room. What did they eat? Were there babies? Did the mouse family migrate to a new barn, thanks to my truck?

"Life moves pretty fast. If you don't stop and look around once in a while, you could miss it." —Ferris Bueller.

After all these years, exploring wildlife habitat still fascinates me. I'm enjoying the moment when it dawns on me, that from this tiny nest inside of my bigger one, it's a perfect moment in time. Nose bleed and all.

LOOKING FOR A SIGN

When the autumn time-change happens, I always feel like my house gets smaller—by a few acres. The outside is my favorite room and I resent winter for taking it from me.

And is it just me, or is every winter somehow a bit more twisted and confused than the one before? In the dark months, everything on the prairie seems the literal definition of *the dead of winter*. It's a monotone landscape, flat-cold, with barely a tree to distract my sullen gaze.

And just when three layers of clothing feels like enough, the wind kicks in like a boat-load of drunken pirates, cursing and careening across the farm, blowing off any hope the snow might give for a green spring. The wind leaves a snow desert, frozen and parched. It makes us all twitchy.

"The wind shows us how close to the edge we are." —Joan Didion.

This winter I had the added distraction of a frozen water hydrant in the barn, but just the last six weeks or so. Still, it isn't like I had to haul buckets of water to the herd in the howling wind. I just had to drain the hose from the barn to the far side of the house in the howling wind.

I start to look for a sign in January. It's way too early for a hint of spring, but I generally have some free time in January. The days begin to lengthen, just a minute at a time and I watch...

I know better than to listen to the weather guy, and calendars are out of touch with reality. It's smarter to take a cue from the animals.

43

Watch the barometric horse—every herd has one—they let you know when a storm is on the way. It's sometimes colic discomfort, or colitis. Sometimes it's just a blunt refusal at turnout time, "No, thanks. I'm fine right here."

Winter lingers, and our duck, Fred, is lonely and sad. It's his first winter without Ethel. He waddles out to the pond to check for a thaw, but returns to bathe in his half-frozen, duck-sized feed tub. He can hear the Canada geese flying over.

Then one day something strange happens. It's almost disorienting; the sun feels warm on my back. Temps aren't above freezing but it's been so long since the sun gave up anything more than daylight. Instantly, every animal is flat on the ground like oiled-up sunbathers at the pool.

The next week the temperature shoots all the way up to 37 degrees. The llama girls do an ancient ritual dance of—let's call it love—with each other. That's all I'll say.

An invasion of robins and mountain bluebirds followed.

Then yesterday, the Grandfather Horse led a breakout. It is heart-stopping, literally, to watch a dead-lame horse lift himself up for his Annual Spring Canter. Will his legs hold him? The others followed and everybody got to run on tippy-toes and flag their tails. It didn't last long, and the Grandfather led them all back into their pen for water soon enough. Still, his crime spree is an undeniable rite of spring, including the joint-aching hangover the next day.

"Every spring is the only spring—a perpetual astonishment."
—Ellis Peters

And finally, last to give in, the barn hydrant thawed out. We all survived winter. It's a miracle! Let the hose dragging stop and gimme back that hour of light! Hibernation's over; it's Daylight Savings Saturday night.

EDGAR RICE BURRO'S THEATRICAL DEBUT

… and a donkey's advice for the *real life* dressage world.

We're just home from Edgar Rice Burro's debut in the dramatic presentation of "The Laonia Gold Mining Company" at the Travel Port Campground and Mini Storage, in Lake George, Colorado. (I do not make this stuff up.)

The Friends of the Lake George Library have been writing and producing melodramas—and cooking dinner to serve between acts—for nineteen years! Tickets always sell out early. Traditionally, the plots include silly men, fallen women, and a murder. The audience responds with moans, groans, hisses, and cheers.

I've mentioned Edgar's star quality before. He gets his share of international performance requests, but Edgar doesn't fly. And some of Edgar's best friends are librarians, so he was happy to say yes to Lake George, population 998.

With an understated flair for over-acting, Edgar played Fluffy, donkey confidante and companion to Harriet, aka Dirty Harry. Dirty Harry is a stinky, marginally-domesticated prospector who might be a decent shot if she's sober and wearing her glasses, but that's only conjecture.

The play opens outside the saloon with Dirty Harry and Fluffy greeting stock holders in the Laonia Gold Company.

Dirty Harry drapes an arm around Fluffy's neck, with a blacked-out tooth and a booming voice calls out, "Would you like to pet my ass?"

It probably goes without saying that Edgar's performance was outstanding. He carried a dramatic gravitas, and clearly won the respect of his leading lady, as well as every person attending, since they had to get past him to enter.

Initially I wondered if Edgar would get a touch of stage nerves working with a leading lady who was loud, dirty, blunt, and laughed too much. But he seemed…well… totally at home. Go figure.

Each time a group would make their way past and enter the saloon, Edgar would lift his spectacular ears upright to scan the parking lot for the next victims. Dirty Harry kept the carrots coming. Edgar had the very best time.

I did notice that more women than men agreed to pet Dirty Harry's fluffy ass (or is it ass, Fluffy?) It's okay; perhaps men were more intimidated by this level of talent. Either way, you can never hear too many ass jokes. One attendee got the jump on Dirty Harry when he rushed to kiss Fluffy on the forehead and blurt out, "I kissed your ass." It was that sort of crowd.

Thanks to the Friends of the Lake George Library for including us in their play (double entendre intended). Libraries are true democracies—free and open for the education and enrichment of all. This particular library must be something special to inspire this sort of behavior for almost twenty years. My cheeks hurt from smiling; an evening like this makes me proud of all of us. God Bless America!

Thanks to our friends at Bear Track Ranch and their good mule, Sully. They took excellent care of Edgar during his Lake George visit. We brought Edgar home to our little dressage barn after closing night and he brayed mightily, happy to be reunited with his pet Andalusian. Edgar is kind to horses, even if they aren't very bright.

There was a horrible quiet when Edgar was away. We

missed his good morning bray, his moonlight yodel, and the caterwauling bellow any time I come to the barn. Or I'm visible in a window. Edgar Rice Burro quite literally sets the tone for Infinity Farm.

The theater world can be a pretty elite place, but we loved the warmth shared at the Travel Port Campground and Mini Storage, in Lake George, Colorado, just as much as everyone there loved Edgar. The Friends of the Lake George Library theater group are totally serious about being light-hearted.

My career years have been in the art world and the horse industry; the pretentious manner that can exist in either culture still leaves me ice cold every single time. Since when does rudeness pass for a love of art or horses? Since when should judgment pass for knowledge?

From the outside, the dressage world can seem especially stuffy and elite; some say it's a sport for rich dilettantes. I still believe that dressage training is the best possible path for any horse and rider. I notice lots of us *real life* dressage riders wear dirty breeches and old boots and laugh at ourselves often. The effort and care we give our horses is what's truly elite, and we're humbled by all that our horses give back.

Comes a day that the ostentatious part of the horse world gets you down, come on over to Infinity Farm, where we make fun of pretensions. And Friend, you can pet my ass.

LOVE PLUS FEAR EQUALS CONFIDENCE

It starts pretty much the same way for most of us: One day we see a horse. He's beautiful and free, with an improbable balance of pride and humility. He seems comfortable with his perfection. Most people can just go on about their business as if nothing has happened.

Some of us are never the same. We might be five or forty-five, but something inside swells with love while common sense shrinks proportionally. You can rest your hand on his strong neck and smell his mane. He might lean close and share his breath, in trade for an exhale of yours. It is almost imperceptible, the feel of the hook as it is set deeply and permanently. Connection. It's almost that simple.

Then it's time to ride. One of my clients related her first ride this way: She had waited fifty years, loving horses and longing, waiting, and wanting. She knew *exactly* how glorious it would feel to be carried by a horse. Finally, an acquaintance offered her a ride. And in the arena, with a mounting block and someone holding the horse, she swung her leg over and eased into the saddle. In that perfect moment, she was blindsided with a paralyzing fear.

Some of us ride for months before we get frightened and think twice. Or ride our whole lives, coming off now and then, but don't give it a thought until we get hurt. Or we get older and eventually gravity just exerts a different sort of pull, if we are honest about mortality.

Sometimes a client's husband will confide in me, shaking his head like it's a strange and mystical secret, that his wife is afraid of her horse. Why does she do it? How crazy is that? I give him the truth: Because she can't *not* do it. Then I remind him that it's kind of cheap talk from a spectator, when your feet are firmly in control of the earth.

Riders are all somewhere on this continuum—a tightrope between love and fear. Which is perfect because horses have a fear/flight response, and are on the same tightrope themselves. It's a great place to begin a partnership.

Acknowledging vulnerability can be a strength.

What if fear isn't wrong? It shouldn't have a bad reputation; fear might be another word for respect. No reason to deny it, I think there's a lot of power in calling fear out! Broad daylight has a way of diminishing things that live in the shadows. Fear is the first ingredient in courage, so give fear a measured acknowledgment and keep breathing. Then make some room for accomplishment, too.

Fear can actually improve riding. I think a bit of self-preservation and common sense makes for a good rider, and a measure of fear means that you are aware in the moment, and challenging your horse. A complacent horse might be the most dangerous horse of all.

Making friends with fear is a challenge, but it's still much easier than quitting horses would ever be. So, we ask for forward from our horse, on the ground and in the saddle, even as we ask for forward of ourselves, to move through mental obstacles and doubt.

"The spiritual journey involves going beyond hope and fear, stepping into unknown territory, continually moving forward. The most important aspect of being on the spiritual path may be to just keep moving." —Pema Chödrön

Horses and humans are a mixed bag of beauty and fear, freedom and resistance. The perfect yin-yang path to confidence. The secret is remembering where it all started. The love of horses is a renewable energy source. Forever.

HORSE TRADING AND ONLINE DATING

My grandfather Percy Blake was a horse trader. They say he had a good eye, but I could never quite discern if he was honest or not. Folks respected him but he may have had more income than scruples. Being a horse trader wasn't a black and white thing at that point in history, and it probably hasn't changed much in the hundred years since.

There's still a lot of horse trading going on and sometimes there's a suspension of disbelief between the ad and the genuine article. I compare horse shopping favorably to online dating. And it's the only date that you want a chaperone along—like a trainer who has been around a bit—if you know what I mean.

A word about truth in advertising: I want to believe folks are basically honest. I want to, really, but that would be nuts. It isn't like we all speak the same English language, after all.

Some words seem to have definitions that confuse me. Like the word *bombproof,* for instance. Could it mean that the horse can destroy his tack, the whole trailer, and your bank account, but still be in one piece after a lengthy vet stay?

Needs experienced rider is confusing terminology. I am fairly certain that means the horse has been trained, but is he trained to buck, bolt, or quit? Would that be just the specialty you are seeking, to broaden your range of riding experience maybe?

And *sixteen hands* means… well, who really agrees on that? Perhaps actual height is a proportional measurement, judged on a sliding scale, depending on the height of the seller. Or something.

Just like dating, you can tell if the horse is dead wrong but you can't always tell if he is Mr. Right. It's easy to turn cynical, especially if it's past midnight, and you've been eating chocolate and stalking online sites like Dreamhorse for a few hours. Too many times a would-be rock star ends up being a post-retirement gardener. How old do you suppose that photo is, anyway?

Here are a couple of dating tips: If the ad has too many ancient win photos and pontificates about dozens of accomplishments—or shows baby pictures and calls the weanling a prospect for steeple chase, dressage, Western pleasure and vaulting... it might sound too good to be true. Well, don't trust the seller; he's trying too hard. We've all dated this guy. Once. It was plenty. (The horse might be okay.)

Or maybe the ad sounds interesting and when you call, the seller goes into excruciating detail about every mistake the horse ever made. He has answered the previous ad too many times in his past, and is going to be brutally truthful, recollecting every marginal result or youthful transgression. It's like the guy who tells you about every woman who ever did him wrong, and they all did. (The horse might be okay.)

My favorite ad is the one with a simple description, and photos or a video that is under-produced. The seller has the horse groomed when you arrive and after tacking up, takes him through his paces in a simple way.

Then the buyer mounts and the horse tells us who he is. And sometimes it's like déjà vu. He's romantic; it's like you've known each other forever, you laugh at the same things, and you trust him right away.

Then be objective, try to talk yourself out of it. He is too young, too tall, not at all what you were looking for. Try to make him wrong. But the horse has made his decision. He carries you lightly, he's responsive and relaxed. He snuffles your hair. And you start emailing photos of him to friends who really don't care. It isn't that you can't see his shortcomings, they just don't matter.

I recommend a short engagement, health tests, and a pre-nup

stating he can have all your money. Then get hitched right away. Start the process of growing imperfectly older together.

The other term for that is *happily ever after*.

DUCK DRESSAGE

My ducks are growing up and they need a hobby. Dressage seems the obvious choice; it's what most of us do here. Dressage has an elite, almost aristocratic elegance that the ducks might appreciate.

Duck Dressage has a lot going in its favor: no abusive shoeing practices for their webbies. No nasty rollkur, (hyperflexion of a horse's neck), since a duck bill can't actually get behind the vertical. Come to think of it, none of the other questionable training "aids" work either. That's all fine; I train old school—nothing but peas.

Earlier this summer the herd at Infinity Farm got a new flock. (Actually a group of ducks is called a brace, but I don't like to use that term around horses.) I complimented a friend's Cayoga ducks. They are a beautiful black with iridescent green, purple and blue feathers—the black opals of the duck world. A while later, my friend called to let me know she had a surprise for me—a dozen three-day-old duckies!

They were tiny. As I loaded them one by one into a cat carrier to bring them home, they scurried to huddle in a tight ball. All except for one duck who turned his little body away from the huddle and towards me. He turned his beak to the side, one eye stared right at my face, and he quacked fearlessly. A tirade continued, which I couldn't help but take note of. I shall call him Henri, pronounced *ornery*. He still speaks for the group today.

Once at home, they had to stay inside over-night, but then

on warm days, they traveled in a bucket to duck turnout. I think ducks have the same range of vision that horses have; they are just more honest about it. They all had the one-eyeball stare, turning their beaks to profile gave it a more melodramatic flair. Very effective.

Another of the ducklings was weak; she didn't eat well and if she got wet, she didn't always preen her feathers dry. I nursed her through one especially hard night. I still know who she is, too. She stands back when the peas come out, preferring to not dive into the fray. She knows I will distract the others, and toss her some all for herself. Maybe she's a bit slow, or maybe she's the smart one.

I've been training ducks off and on since I was thirteen years old and taught some mallards to walk the plank. This is my first attempt at duck dressage. Is it crazy? Nah. They have a really strong, or at least big, hind end and quite an elegant neck. Not to mention a ground-covering extended trot when going after bugs.

What would a duck dressage test be like? (Warning: obscure dressage humor ahead.) "A, Enter working waddle. X, Halt and Quack. C, Track right and HXF- Extended Waddle!!

It's truly is a thing of beauty: good webbed break over, lots of push from behind, and an up-hill gait sure to score high, even from the most conservative judge... Okay, maybe individual dressage tests would be silly, even by my standards.

But then it came to me: Quadrille! Ducks would be better suited to quadrille! It's a sure thing. Rose Bowl Parade—here we come.

AUTUMN AND INDOOR SPORTS

It is autumn now. I should be writing poetic essays about geese on the wing, abundant golden harvests, or maybe a symbolic essay about the seasons of life. I'm not in the mood.

Every day the sun comes up later, and goes down earlier. The drought has drained my beautiful pond; my pasture has fried and died. Hay prices are simply impossible. Some of the elder barn residents are struggling already. Am I ready to battle winter again?

Luckily not everyone is the sour-puss I am. After all, these cool nights are bringing more mice into the house. It's kind of like an indoor soccer league for the dogs and cats. They still hunt outside; it's just an extra opportunity, indoors and under the lights.

If it was just cats trapped under the sink, or playing with a mouse in the bathtub, I would just sleep through it. But this is different.

Let the indoor rodent games begin! Our house is about a thousand square feet, patrolled by four dogs and three cats. And they hunt in inter-species packs—a dog and cat together. Not very good odds for rodents. Or lamps. Or glasses of wine poured to distract the writer from mouse murder.

The chase is on—dogs and cats in hot pursuit of small intruders, shoving furniture around to look like random tornado damage. Eventually the action slows, as no one is in any hurry for the inevitable yet. Some mice escape, even now.

The hunters are going for style points; scoring this game is as complicated as a dressage test.

Here's a quote from the feline winner:

***

Tiny? Are you kidding? If you adjust my size to human size, this mouse the equivalent to you bringing down a beagle. Could you manage? I don't think so. Besides, he was very quick and really mean. You're welcome. —Squirrel, Tiny (Medium) Game Hunter.

***

Barn mice really seem tougher than these seasonal intruders. Or maybe the mice that migrate to the house in winter are snowbird mice, looking for a warm place to retire. Sorry, our house is no mouse Miami.

Back when I was new to this indoor blood sport, one of the cats brought a big fat vole in the house and put him on the kitchen counter. A vole the size of a kitten, with only a few puncture wounds and very much alive.

I've had enough mice fly out of the grain bin and into my face that I'm not rodent shy. But this job did seem to require more than a tissue. I put the cat on the floor and grabbed some Tupperware from the dish drain. In the blink that I looked away, the vole disappeared. Simultaneously Howdy, the dog, tried to quietly exit the room. He was so very nonchalant; he might have whistled if there wasn't a very live vole in his mouth.

Yikes, I dove to the dog and pried his jaw open. No time to chew, no vole, but the dog looked suspicious. Had he swallowed the vole whole? It got immediately quiet. My dog looked at me and I looked at him. One of us was more squinty-eyed than the other.

How long could the un-chewed vole hold his breath inside

my dog? Would the vole try to escape? Or were vital organs being shredded by that mad vole's nasty toenails? I continued watching my dog, who continued to watch me.

It wasn't the end of the world for most of us. I didn't fund a new wing at the emergency vet hospital. But Howdy did have pretty nasty gas the next day.

Is this mouse blood-sport cruel? No more so than dust bowl droughts or old horses facing winter. This Circle of Life has some dark parts. Suck it up.

BEWARE: COLIC SEASON

She was lying flat; eyes closed, flank tense and very quiet. As I got closer I could see lots of ragged hoof marks on the ground. Are you thinking what I am?

It's Windy. She was something in the day, but now she's a well-worn twenty-two years old, with a suitcase of maladies. Like an old woman, she gets tinier each year. And now she was in gut wrenching pain—her muscles tell the story.

Is it the dreaded "C" word? I waited for the vet and did a poop chant silently.

Colic is my sworn enemy, the number one killer of horses, and its cause is still somewhat nebulous. It can be caused by a weather change, a rapid barometer jump, or a slow shift of season. Or a change of feed, or a trailer ride. Dehydration. Ulcers. Heat cycles. Sand. Horses have such a sensitive digestive system; the truth is that any change can do it.

My vet arrived fresh from other colic calls, and performed the usual protocol: pain meds, rectal exam, tube down the nose to the stomach. She loves that part. Her heart rate was too low, she was too exhausted, and she was hardly able to stand. He gave me the directions for care. (One of my other horses had chronic colic issues, five or six times a month for over two years, so I'm very familiar.)

And he said there was some sand. Sand gets ingested from eating off the ground, which is pretty hard to avoid ultimately. It's especially common in older horses like Windy, and with the drought locally, there's more dirt and less grass. I know all this, so I'd done a big psyllium supplement purge last month. Which apparently did not do the trick, we are on a month-long purge now. I make a note; if Windy is struggling, the Grandfather Horse probably needs a longer purge, too.

I optimistically ask about what's new on the horizon for colic treatment. The vet told me that there are better tests now to tell sooner if your horse needs surgery. Quicker to surgery is good, but my sweet Windy was not a surgery candidate. At this age, and with other health questions, it wouldn't be kind.

Is your horse a surgery candidate? It's good to make that decision on a day that your horse is peacefully grazing in the pasture. Emergencies are emotional times and it isn't always the right choice. If your horse is elderly, the surgery is extensive and can be pretty hard on them. Not everyone has insurance and the surgery runs between $7,000 and $14,000. If surgery isn't right for your horse, you might practice saying it out loud, "My horse is not a surgery candidate." Sometimes physically saying it is the hardest part when emotions are high during an emergency.

Windy's result was good. The vet said it was a mild colic. (Doesn't fatal colic start that way?) I continued the poop chant, but twenty-four hours passed with no result. Recovery was very slow. She is cautiously okay now, but the colic took a toll; she is thinner, depressed, and still exhausted.

On a separate but related note, yesterday morning I was driving to a lesson with a new client and thinking about writing this. My stomach was kind of twitchy. If I was a horse, you would call me stoic; I soldier on. We spent an hour evaluating and working with her horse. The lesson went well, we talked about perception and the art of release. The rider had invited another potential client to watch.

We were just finishing and ...my gut seized. Reflex quick, I threw up on the center line of her arena. I never do this, I'm that sort who is never sick, and it wasn't remotely graceful. It was really nice footing too. Awkward! I just wasn't sure what the polite comment from me should be. Was is food poisoning? Flu? Or maybe colic, and I'm actually turning into a horse? Would that be enlightenment?

My client asked if I throw up often, and I shook my head. And immediately threw up again. I think her dog felt sorry for me. Humility—it never gets old.

I was fine a few hours later but then my old dog threw up all night. It was an epidemic!

We are expecting our first snow of the season on our Colorado prairie tonight. Maybe an extra walk-through before bed to double-check the water and throw extra hay with a special eye on the herd elders. Here's wishing everyone a soft stomach and a gentle winter.

PONY SMART AND CARROT SHY

Breezy was a small pinto pony who came to my client's barn as part of a real estate deal. A friend of theirs couldn't close the sale of their property unless the pony was gone and my clients had room with their other horses. In the beginning, Breezy was a favorite with the neighborhood kids. Somehow over time, he became more and more fearful until he was impossible to catch. That's where I came in.

Breezy was almost too handsome; a black and white pinto with wild blue eyes. As I watched him, the owner told me her family had tried. Their daughter was a teen rider who did her best. The dad had played with him some, but after hearing the description of their game… well, good intention but a dangerous miscommunication. Then two different horse-people had offered to help, each saying it would be an easy job. The pony was just a little spoiled was all. Eventually both people gave up in turn, having done more damage than good, leaving Breezy frightened and untouchable. By now his hooves were at least an inch too long with huge chunks broken out. He'd lost all trust in humans.

Breezy faced me head on and his eyes did not blink. Ever. They were so round and tense that I thought they might pop right out of his head. As I stepped to one side, his hind legs crossed over, pivoting—twisting—his front hooves, but never releasing eye contact or his full-frontal position. His body was tight, every molecule braced. He used no calming signals; he was shut down and over-stimulated all at once. During the next hour, I didn't make much headway but I was hooked.

It was a training quandary: I didn't think he'd be a quick re-train and ponies don't cost less to work with than full-sized horses. I asked if my client might consider relinquishing him to a rescue because the process was going to be costly. I was thinking perhaps I could foster him, as I had other ponies, until the kinks got worked out. But the owner said no; Breezy was their responsibility and they'd pay his bills. She hoped I'd take him on. So now I have serious respect for this hand-me-down pony owner.

In a few days, I was back to help load him into their trailer. Breezy was in a stall when I arrived, so haltering him only took a little over an hour and by mid-afternoon he was in one of my runs, his backside wedged into a corner and facing me with all his might. Breezy didn't drink and he ignored his hay. I never saw him eat once that first month, but I refilled his hay bin every day. Mucking his pen was a slow and quiet job.

And we had stare-downs. One day I took an apple in with me, ate a bite or two, and offered the rest to Breezy at a distance. He panicked and did a rearing spin, and then bolted past me. I lowered my eyes and exhaled an apology, while he quivered at the end of the run. So, that was how they tried to catch him. Horses will tell you everything.

Was he abused? Some people thought so but I wasn't so sure. It didn't matter; Breezy thought he had been and that was the only opinion that counted. When horses take something to heart, they're no different from us. I didn't threaten him with fruit again. I know it sounds crazy, but for all his avoidance, I always knew he was fighting to find his way back.

Change came slowly. Haltering was possible if he was in his *safe* corner and I breathed more than I moved. Weeks later, I was able to pick up his feet, but touching his body remained impossible. Still no blinking, but I found a way to use our stare-downs in his favor. I'd take a step to the left and his head followed me, and then the same step to the right. I did this passive two-step back and forth, again and again, and twenty minutes of neck sway later, his poll seemed to relax a bit and he blinked. So did I.

Here's where I share my favorite training aid. Some swear by clickers or flags, and a well-timed piece of carrot can be a miracle. Because horses are all a bit different, there's no one thing that always works. I'll always believe the best aid available is our own creativity.

We continued that warm-up every day, followed by some obstacles in hand. He was totally fearless marching through the llama pen and the plastic wading pool. He matched my stride on a slack line, but if he felt a hint of pressure on the rope, he sat back violently. People remained his biggest fear.

At the end of our session, I'd slowly step to his shoulder. I gradually touched his neck more in the process of loosening his halter, just an inch a week. Eventually my hand made its way to his back. His body felt like plywood. His muscles were so tight that even his skin was stiff. Touch terrified him, but every day he tried to tolerate more.

Breezy was a hard case; I respected that. By the time a year passed, the farrier could trim him if she hummed and made no sudden moves. I could hand groom him but some currycombs and brushes were still too much. He was far from okay but he couldn't stay forever. I asked his owners if I might try to find him a suitable home.

A couple of weeks later I got a call about a companion horse and after a complicated conversation, I invited the caller to my farm. Breezy was in the round pen when she arrived and I asked if she'd like to go in. I'd been brutally truthful on the phone, but she still looked surprised when Breezy bolted away from a small boy who walked up. She spoke in a sweet high voice and reached toward him, but he acted like she'd cracked a bull whip. That was the moment Breezy went beyond cute and became interesting. She listened and took her groundwork down a notch, and then even quieter. A half hour later, both Breezy and

I were impressed and the two of them struck a deal.

I got updates frequently during his first year with her. There was a wonderful photo of Breezy, standing dwarfed between her two Thoroughbreds, and still the proud herd leader. His new owner gushed about his progress and renamed him Joey Try. Finally, she told me that after some months of watching her other two geldings chew contentedly on theirs, this brave pony was able to accept a carrot from her hand.

Training is an art and human logic doesn't always rule. Sometimes carrots are complicated. Then other times, they're just sweet.

FARM POLITICS: IT TAKES ALL KINDS

Here at Infinity Farm, we have all kinds. In fact, we have inter-species chaos.

I want to affirm that I like order. But I'm the minority here, so not everyone goes along with my Type-A fantasies. Exactly like real life, we don't all fit into little boxes.

Sure, I have some level of leadership out of the saddle. After all, I have opposable thumbs, so I have the gate advantage. Except for Edgar Rice Burro, who has opposable lips.

So, Infinity Farm is a democracy. That means we have politics; the lively discussion of policy and the art of compromise. Anyone with contrary cats, goats, or donkeys knows that a rule by consensus is the best you can get. It's a bit complicated, again, exactly like real life.

Maybe my gelding Dodger started it. He has been gone five years this week; we still miss his Ivy League class and sense of humor. Dodger was gay. He was born that way, we all knew. He ignored all mares but was very flirtatious with chestnut geldings. Our most common judge's comment: Happy Horse. As it should be.

Then there's the orange cat Lulu who sleeps on top of Tomboy, the Briard, and purrs like a Harley. I mean every day, on the sofa or out in the yard. It's an up/down thing, but they are committed. Do you know couples like that?

Finny, the dog, isn't burdened with deep thoughts; he dreams of pizza crust. Hero, our elder dog, is getting weak, so he starts fights to let us know he's still strong. Howdy, the alpha dog is a loner— better to protect the farm that way. Hank, the cat, has finally aged-out of chasing dogs and coyotes. We hope.

JoeGoat is profoundly attached to Holiday, the llama. I used to think that my fence-building skills were greater than Joe Goat's love for Holiday, but I was wrong. See, JoeGoat was born in the wrong body. He was meant to be a llama all along; he even ignored his twin. It took some convincing but eventually I gave up the fence fight, now JoeGoat lives with Holiday... but it isn't a happy ending. Did I mention Holiday doesn't return the affection? It doesn't matter though, JoeGoat is living a dream but with less hair. Sound familiar?

Sebastian, another llama, loves redheaded women with honey-colored skin. I have learned his type through necessity. I've had to warn women that Seb has a poor sense of personal space. He must be very close while inhaling their breath and smacking his lips. Is this harassment?

And then there is Edgar Rice Burro, and Clara, my young mare. They groom each other for hours, until they are literally covered with spit. I can't say I like her hanging around with someone of his age and experience, but no one is immune to a donkey's charm.

The Grandfather Horse thinks he is the king of the world. He's absolutely right.

There's Nubè, a mid-life gelding who seems almost idiot-savant strange and has extreme ulcers to match. I wonder if horses have autism; the vets don't have a better answer. One mare has an equine version of post-traumatic stress, but her trust in us grows at a glacial pace. Is it too late for her? The elderly matriarch of the herd tries to be invisible, and yet is so pleased when you notice her. And the Dude Rancher calls our relationship "three degrees off true north." That sounds about right.

At the end of the day, I am surprised at how much everyone here wants to get along. Celebrate diversity and pass the cookies.

"Life is just a short walk from the cradle to the grave, and it

sure behooves us to be kind to one another along the way." —Alice Childress.

Infinity Farm is a micro version of this country. Americans are a proud and rowdy bunch of individuals, too. Freedom can look civilized and chaotic at the same time, but keep in the game—even if the politics make you crazy. For all the off-beat weirdness, it still takes all kinds to get it right.

HOW TO GET A STINKY OLD DOG

Puppy breath is one of those addictive smells that isn't actually pleasing aromatically. Still, who doesn't inch their nose dangerously close to those tiny razor teeth, just for a whiff?

One bright Sunday morning while driving to the barn to ride, I saw a sign on a ranch gate: *Heeler Pups.* I'd recently lost an elderly dog—I think he might have turned the wheel—but there I was, looking at a litter of vampire puppies with pointy little ears and those dangerous teeth! A pale-colored one was sitting quietly to the side, staring me right in the eye. He seemed sincere. I shook my head, got back in my truck, and left for the barn.

Four hours later, my truck turned into the ranch driveway again. Some of the pups were gone, but the pale one was still in the same spot, with the same quiet eye contact. He looked like a young James Dean. I picked him up this time, brought him close and took a big whiff. His breath was exquisite. We each made a choice and never looked back.

"There is honor in being a dog." —Aristotle.

My life was in a nose-dive of a midlife crisis at the time: I named him Hero. It was a big name for a little pup but that was what I needed. I could rattle off dozens of stories of his courage and wit, but let it stand: Hero is *my dog.* Enough said.

That's how I got my stinky old dog; it takes about fourteen years for the smell to fully ripen.

And yes, the stink is from his mouth. He has a few abscesses, a broken canine tooth. My good vet gives me a bi-annual course of antibiotics for him. His teeth aren't the priority.

A few times a day, Hero follows me into the bathroom. There is a chair in there that's lower to the ground than other chairs in the house. He turns his bony self in a half circle and backs up to sit between my feet. He leans into me, extends his nose straight up as I fold him in my arms. We rest there a good while. Hero has never been the sort to worry about the future.

I can't help it, one hand slides down to his heart. It's beating big. Enlarged is the word the vet used. The diagnosis progressed over time to End Stage Heart Failure, and Hero got a hall pass from any more vet visits. No more teeth cleaning, no more shots. Kind of good news if you look at it that way.

Some folks drag their pets through every medical procedure available to fight the inevitable. It isn't a crime to get old and I don't want Hero thinking he's failing me somehow. Each day is good enough.

Hero is asleep on a memory foam bed under my desk as I write. There's a space heater keeping us happy. He's become a heavy sleeper now; it's the upside of being stone deaf.

Sometimes Hero falls over. His blood pressure drops and he loses consciousness briefly. But then he blinks his eyes a few times and braces his body to stand. It doesn't ruin his day, so I don't let it ruin mine.

Hero doesn't want us to know he is getting weaker, so he starts more fights with the big dogs who live here. Sometimes he barks just in case there's a reason that he can't hear. He has a fine tenor bark.

Did I mention it has been more than twenty months since the "end stage" term was first used? Hero doesn't want your sympathy. Nothing here is bad or wrong...

"Dogs lives are too short...their only fault, really." -Agnes Sligh Turnbull.

Friday nights are movie night, and there's a spot on the couch between the Dude Rancher and me that's just big enough for a stinky old dog. He's all elbows and toenails until he settles in, heaving a satisfied sigh. If love has a smell, this is it.

MUCKING FOR PEACE

Thanksgiving is my favorite holiday. I think we should nix all the others and just celebrate Thanksgiving. Once a month would be good. I'd be fine with changing the meal sometimes, as long as the sacred tradition of eating too much, sleeping, and saying thank you was still the order of the day. You've got to love a holiday with such low expectations.

And I have so much to be grateful for. Today, as I took a deep breath, quieting outside distractions, I heard a still, small voice from very deep inside of me say, "I hate everybody." Usually I stay belligerently positive; I have a pretty wonderful life. But sometimes I get the Over-stressed/Under-appreciated Flu. Ever had it? You catch it from people, not horses.

Lucky for me, I have the cure right at hand. It's salvation in the form of a muck fork and cart. There's some sort of universal balance struck between human emotional excrement and the actual muck created by horses.

Some days it's a quick fix, just tidying one stall delivers easy satisfaction. But today will require an entire herd's muck at the minimum. With another dose in twenty-four hours.

The first and best thing about muck is that you find it in the vicinity of horses. Once you're in the pen, you don't have to start right away. You could have a lean on an old horse soaking in the sun and try to remember why you didn't name him Prozac twenty-five years ago.

You can fill your lungs, rant to the sky, and let the prairie wind carry the anger away, along with the lawn chairs, feed buckets, and anything else not tied down. After a few forkfuls tossed into the cart, my shoulders start to melt away from my ears and there's an illusion that order is being restored to the universe, one pile at a time.

Wait! I know what you're thinking, and I'm so sorry. I only have seven horses, one donkey, four llamas and two goats; and with my own mental health needs, I just don't have one extra turd to spare. I really can't invite you over for a mental health muck-visit. Maybe you could volunteer at a horse rescue?

And so, on I muck from horse to horse. Windy likes a quiet hand on her shoulder. Grace holds back, but her bright eyes follow every step. Nubè likes to wrap me up with his neck, while Clara prefers to share her breath.

There's a donkey who totally obscures my view every day by managing to keep his body between me and the muck cart. I've gotten good at trick shots—maybe a twisting overhead lob. Hoop-ilicious! The manure has air time and I wait for it… Swish! My donkey-blind poop lands mostly in the cart and Edgar Rice Burro congratulates me with an ear scratch. His ears, of course.

My personal mental health plan is to keep on mucking until the days are long again, the sun is warm again, and people learn to at least *mimic* their horse's kindness and grace. I know I'll have to settle for two out of three, but with enough muck time, I can make that work.

Eventually I muck my way to a full cart at the far corner of the property. I do a combination bench press/belly bump to empty the muck, the barn equivalent of a clean and jerk movement. And as I shake the last of the muck out, my eyes survey all that is mine. We are a plain little barn. No false fronts, no secret agendas, no hidden muck. Just a multifarious herd of good souls who are forever grateful for a scratch and a kind word.

Acknowledgment is all any of us want.

FAMILY SUCH AS WE ARE

The holiday season is upon us. From Thanksgiving till the end of the year, we're encouraged to celebrate the family, seen through Norman Rockwell eyes. Lots of us fit that mold. Our families come together, smile into the camera, and stay up late laughing. Generations of women gather in kitchens and cook massive meals to the praise of the men folk.

But some of us didn't come from warm families. Some of us had parents who didn't really want kids after all. Some of us have lost loved ones, or are living apart. Some of us are unwanted members of an extended family. Some of us are just in-between and awkward about it. And some of us are flat-out lonely.

Each year we smile and accept holiday invitations from gracious friends whose families make us feel welcome. It's a wonderful to share holiday time, but then during a toast, we might feel we've fallen short of *normal* somehow. Do you know all the words to *Blue Christmas*? Have you had that long drive home in the dark?

Where do you start if you want a family of your own, but people don't seem to be cooperating? How do you recuperate if you have taken a bounce or two, and aren't as confident or trusting as before?

One gift animals give us is a place to keep our hearts, safe and secure, until we can find a place to merge back with our own species.

Can you get a cat? You can learn a lot about self-esteem from a cat. They have an enviable way of taking care of themselves first and feeling good about it.

Horses are the best teachers for learning to grow trust and honesty, it's their first language. Plus, they can lift you up and carry you to a better place, in more ways than you can imagine.

And if you need some love without conditions or limitations (who doesn't?), then the obvious answer is a dog. Dogs aren't burdened with the full range of emotions, so their understanding of unconditional love is much more evolved than ours.

I'm not suggesting that you dress all your animals up in little matching sailor suits and make them eat at the table with you. I think if you have more than forty or fifty cats it might be time to ask yourself some hard questions. And I'm not proposing a constitutional amendment for inter-species marriage.

But life is complicated. People can come and go, and for some of us, family connections are not always dependable. Sometimes a little creativity in defining family can make all the difference.

Now I'm an old gray mare and grateful for my acquired family of humans. And I'm forever grateful for the fur family that cared for me before I found my home, and for the ones who still stand guard for me now.

Does your family include more than one species? From before Noah's Ark and still today, some members of the family were always supposed to have fur, or feathers, or eek, even scales. I think that was always the plan.

A LITTLE LLAMA LIFE

We have a fairly healthy herd here at Infinity Farm. We're eight species strong, mostly horses, but we have our fair share of ruminants as well. Sometimes you can pick up a sick vibe from the herd before you can figure out which animal it is. It could be someone not in their usual place or even a missing sound you can't put your finger on. This week it was a llama who stood around the hay with the others. It wasn't immediately obvious that she wasn't actually eating.

Her real name is Belle Starr, but she's what my people call a big boned girl so it's hard to not refer to her as the Belly Llama. She had a bit of a digestive upset that I could set right with probiotics and a minimum of syringe wrestling. She's fine now, but I got to remembering her little sister, Clementine.

Clemmie was a huge cria. She hit the ground strong and tall. She looked a month old on day two, with soft honey-brown curls and a fluid confident step. Clementine was a quick learner, brave enough to separate from the herd, and so strong by the time she was two, that I started training her to drive. Clemmie was a natural. But by the time Clemmie was three, she started losing weight. It wasn't so noticeable at first, but the more I tried to get weight on her, the more she lost.

I have a good llama vet; we did a series of tests. All her numbers were good. The vet said that if she hadn't *seen* Clemmie, she would say she was the healthiest llama around. Over the next year, Clemmie got very frail. Nothing we tried helped, but the vet didn't think she was in pain. Everyone in the herd was gentle with her and summer was coming, so I just let her have time.

You know this part: One day she seemed different. Clemmie didn't want to eat and she couldn't balance to stand up. The other llamas were staying closer than usual. It seemed this might be the day, and I made the call for Clemmie one last time. The llama vet promised to come as soon as possible.

An hour passed. Clemmie struggled to hold her head up, she'd lost her equilibrium. But it was harder for her to breathe if she laid it down. Her lungs sounded congested so I sat down and held her head so she could be more comfortable. No vet yet, but the horses had joined the other llamas, all standing in a loose arc around us, quietly watching Clemmie.

Another hour passed and no vet truck yet. Clemmie was breathing easier with me holding her head, but she was weaker and her breaths shallower. Now the goats and donkeys had joined the horses and llamas holding vigil. The dogs were lying down and watching from a distance. Everyone was in a respect-ful circle around me and Clemmie, waiting and breathing in a peaceable way.

"*The most precious gift we can offer others is our presence. When mindfulness embraces those we love, they will bloom like flowers.*" —Thich Nhat Hanh.

Another half hour and the dogs don't bark, but I finally heard the truck. My vet hurried over and confirmed what all of us knew. In a kind moment, Clementine was released.

There might have been a collective sigh but it was probably just me. Eventually, one by one, the herd began to wander away. Some sniffed Clemmie. The llamas stayed close to each other. My Grandfather Horse was the last to leave.

Clementine had a little life. She's been gone several years now. Do they ever remember her? The herd circle still comes together for special occasions, like the full moon night our Clara was born. Life in our herd goes on, ordinary and special at the same time.

I keep thinking about The Cambridge Declaration on Consciousness, signed by a prestigious crowd of international scientists. There are some very big words explaining that scientists have proved that animals have conscious states similar to humans. Lately, I wish humans had conscious states more similar to animals.

But it's an election year. Know what I mean?

EDGAR RICE BURRO'S THOUGHTS ON PEACE

Disclaimer: I'm going to transcribe for Edgar. Donkeys are very smart, profoundly philosophical, and endowed with Victorian sensibilities. Edgar is prone to never using a small word when several large words are available. He believes public displays, such as speaking in front of groups, are frequently garish. He has agreed to privately share some thoughts for our edification.

***

We donkeys are very smart. Sometimes people consider donkeys a bit coarse. To the insensitive handler, we might appear stubborn. Appearing stubborn is just our response to rudeness. We donkeys have quiet, sensitive hearts and we believe in civilized discourse. We have DonkeyZen.

We donkeys notice humans let their emotions get very big. You're a bit scattered, even, dare I say, unstable. And so very loud! Do you think these ears don't hear?

***

Edgar, take a breath.

***

Sometimes humans swagger into the stable, slamming things around and interrupting everyone's digestion. And that's just with their jangled thoughts. Humans have a plan with a time schedule and they expect everyone in the barn to participate. Excuse me, Human, yeah you, jerking the rope. What makes you think you can barge in the barn and order us around?

It rattles my DonkeyZen. We donkeys hate to fight, even more than horses. It doesn't matter if you humans don't think you're the adversarial ones. It's not for you to judge—that job belongs to those feeling the brunt of your behavior. Take my word for it.

***

Well, he's right. We are the adversarial ones.

***

We donkeys love work, it gives us self-respect and usefulness. Some of my best friends are horses, and they love work even more. We want our human to have a vision, but then negotiate the agenda with us. Just ask us clearly; don't be rude about it. Then take a breath and give me a chance to gather my thoughts before you require an answer. It will take as much time as it takes, but if you rush me, it will take longer.

***

Okay, he's right about that too. We are the impatient ones.

***

And didn't your mother ever teach you to say thank you?

***

Wow. Three for three. Yes, we usually don't get grateful until we lose something.

***

I apologize—a disturbance in my DonkeyZen is no reason to speak poorly of your mother. But it's true, you humans would have your manners improved by partnering with donkeys. I recommend it. Sometimes a horse will give you the benefit of the doubt. Sometimes a horse will allow themselves to be bullied; one of their character flaws, if you ask me. Donkeys like me require humans to be honest and trustworthy for us to consider partnership, and only then do you get our best work. And yes, we are worth it.

***

Bottom line is this: Some humans believe that an equine would never do their work without intimidation and bullying. If this is your method of training, you might not even be evolved enough to partner with a donkey. Your horse might not like you as much as you think he does, either.

Other humans believe that you can invite an equine to work and get a better result. It takes mental connection, sometimes deeper and more honest than handlers have, even with other humans.

***

You humans are hard to trust with your unstable temperaments and no real ear to speak of. I think you are basically good creatures.

but you could take a lesson from us. My advice to humans is to cultivate some DonkeyZen of your own. Like Mother Teresa says, "If we have no peace, it is because we have forgotten that we belong to each other."

***

Well, Edgar is right; quiet wisdom of donkeys has been in the stable since the first Christmas for good reason, and the message bears repeating. *Peace on Earth. Goodwill to all God's creatures.*

NEW YEAR'S DAY, MINUS THE HAPPY

It was New Year's Eve, and I was listening to a sad radio memorial about the musicians who passed this year. I do the same thing on my farm at year end; I take a census and remember my losses.

We lost a wonderful goat this year. Elvis loved flirting with women, sleeping with his twin, Sumo, and masterminding escapes. Sumo still mourns. And a barrage of loud, sarcastic quacking reminds me we're up a dozen ducks.

It could have been so much worse; we have an aging population here at Infinity Farm. Both of my elderly horses are frail. On cold days, the Grandfather Horse doesn't want to walk even a few steps. The old mare has colicked twice so far this fall. One of the llamas is eighteen now; I watch her closely as well.

And then there's my cattle dog, Hero, in end stage heart failure for the last two years. Sometimes he seems too tough to die, but it's been a hard couple of weeks with him having more "fainting" spells. I value each moment with this extremely stinky old dog. Hero was sleeping under my desk New Year's Eve, as I was listening to the musician's memorial and writing in my studio.

A few minutes later, I was speeding to the all-night emergency vet clinic with Howdy. Some of you knew him; Howdy usually rode shotgun in my truck. I could tell it was bloat, the canine equivalent of colic. Is there anything worse?

A few minutes after arriving at the ER, I was holding him and signing papers. I think the best part of him was gone already. I told Howdy what a good boy he was, breathing with him as the vet administered the drugs to release him from our life.

And then he was gone. It was like a sonic boom. Such a heart! Empty in a moment. I felt so disoriented that I called our best friend to *talk* me home, but I got lost anyway.

Have you ever had a dog who was so perfect and true that it seemed any words you could use about him would only diminish who he was?

Oh, hell, of course you have. All our dogs are that way. Howdy and I didn't share some unique, sacred trust. What we shared was just normal. And he'd hate me to tell maudlin stories about him. Howdy was just a dog.

Like a horse is just a horse. Meaning he was a fully dimensional sentient being, with emotions and intellect and the ability to commit his whole being, in ways a mere human would struggle to do. It's just that Howdy was *my* dog.

"He will be yours…to the last beat of his heart. You owe it to him to be worthy of such devotion." —Unknown.

Howdy's love was ferocious; it could make you feel pretty special. I'll pay that forward to the next dog. Yes, I'll get another dog soon; it's the best way to honor his memory. Howdy will be irreplaceable, but the mentoring job that he took up from the long line of dogs that came before him must continue. I'll always need the help of a few dogs to improve my natural self.

What I notice is that no matter how much I give to animals, I always get more back. I always wind up ahead of where I started, once I can breathe again, once the first pain of loss begins to heal. It's a special blessing to be owned by a dog; I'm the lucky one.

For now, I'm haunted. I see Howdy in passing shadows and feel his big head in the center of my back, pushing me out of the truck. I want to save his nose prints on the front window.

Maybe you are missing a dog who made you feel special, too.

"Grief is like the ocean; it comes on waves ebbing and flowing.

Sometimes the water is calm, and sometimes it is overwhelming. All we can do is learn to swim." —Vicki Harrison.

But then the sun came up and its New Year's Day. I keep a special eye on my collapsing old cattle dog. And I take care to give the elder horses an extra bedtime snack during this frozen, dark season.

RESCUE ME

I've been in a really lousy mood lately. I've been pondering mortality. The loss of a hard-working dog and a sweet old horse has got me feeling particularly cold and dark this winter.

I'm usually pretty good at picking myself up, but this time it's a lot to lift. I started doing that thing that sad people do late at night on the internet—I started cruising dog rescue websites. I have a confession. I'm attracted to a certain body type. And yes, I like being herded.

Adopting a rescue dog is a strange combination of online dating and an arranged marriage. You pick a picture and profile of someone you like, but it isn't up to you. There's an application with references, and you list your past relationships and how they ended. And who you live with now, and how they feel would feel about a new pack member. The rescue organization acts as a protective mother/matchmaker.

There was a very irresistible old corgi matron with a chunk out of an ear and only one eye in Kansas. She had a list of ailments a mile long, and a cocky tilt to her head. She was a pirate corgi with a certain grace. Adopting older dogs has big rewards, but it wasn't right for me this time.

Finally, I saw him. He was in Wyoming. He and his brother were living like frat boys with a suburban family with two toddlers. Too much barking, too much partying, too much detention in the crate—it was a vicious circle. The brothers went to rescue, truly from too much love, with broken hearts on all sides. And the Matchmaker already had my application.

Road Trip! A friend and I headed north, fueled by caffeine and dog passion. We pulled into an easy-to-find chain restaurant's parking lot in Cheyenne and there he was, acting contrite and nervous, showing a little too much belly and trying way too hard to please. There's an argument that neither the Corgi Boy nor I were all that discerning, but *whatever*. It was love at first sight.

In the car on the way home the Corgi Boy changed his name to Walter. Since deciding to become a contributing member of society, an alias was in order. A few treats and some sweet talk and it was Walter, Walter, Walter.

Walter is working with me in the truck now. He's making new dog friends. There's a claw mark on an ear that lets me know that the curiosity about the cats has been answered. Walter is exhausted. Relentlessly herding me is a full-time job, but he's lost track of a few humans lately and he's not about to take his eyes off me.

His bad habits? They told us Walter barks too much. Well, he frequently makes a deep quacking noise; the Dude Rancher does a good impression of it. And Walter lets out a yodel over the prairie when inspired. He sings to himself most of the time. Not much barking though.

He's developing a taste for beet pulp. Yes, it's horse feed, and in frigid weather, I soak a bucket of it in the bathtub. Yesterday I heard a noise; he managed to lob himself over the edge of the tub and landed high-centered over the top of the bucket. His feet were too short, he was stuck wiggling. In his defense, he showed not one shred of guilt as I lifted him off. He's settling in just fine.

I know that he's herding me close partly because he misses his family in Wyoming. I think he knows I'm missing family, too. It's like this in midlife; we're all adjusting to change and loss.

Dog rescue is a lot like horse rescue. They come in all ages, purebreds and mixed breeds. Some were not cared for and some are given up with great reluctance. Each one is an individual life with a unique story. Each one is willing to rescue you. You just have to ask.

SURVIVING OLD AGE

Can we talk about surviving old age? It isn't mine I'm worried about. It'll catch up without any help from me.

I am more concerned with the herd here at Infinity Farm. We used to positively percolate with vitality and there was a dancing joie *de vivre* here on the windy, treeless prairie. Everyone bounded everywhere.

But now the herd has aged like Baby Boomers, and most of us count our years in double digits. We still have some insolent youth around, but the old horses lean against barns meditating on sunny afternoons. There are llamas with long teeth and crooked toes; their fleeces are coarse as steel wool now. The surviving goats are officially *old* goats. That's different.

The dogs slowly wake up to visitors who are already in the house. And Hank, feline mass murderer of bunnies and rodents, is nearly toothless. Sometimes I wander through the herd, idly predicting which of my hips will get replaced first. It's my personal reminder of the wondrous years we shared. And we are far from done.

Do you ever do the math? When I'm seventy, my young mare will be sixteen. But who else will still be here? The herd will dwindle by attrition; we aren't the sort to send off the elders who can no longer work. The passing of time will do that quickly enough. And so, our family gets a little smaller each year.

I've lost animals suddenly, unexpectedly before their time. It's a wasabi sort of pain, undeniable. Hot and crisp in its bite, a slam of reality. In some ways, it's easier than the pain of gradual erosion.

The slow-motion ache of watching a beloved's life grow dimmer, just a day at a time, is more subtle, but deeper and heavier. I want to enjoy this precious time, but the future is as inevitable as gravity. I must get better at this; I always outlive them.

"Old age is no place for sissies." —Bette Davis.

Boy howdy, that's for sure. I have done some brave and crazy things in this life, but standing toe-to-toe with time takes a strong gut. There will be too many goodbyes in the future.

For all my whining about it, and I *am* whining, the animals don't seem so very concerned. After all, it's the natural progression of things. No one wants plastic surgery or dental restoration. They accept reality and then enjoy lunch. I think horses are Buddhist (and better for it). We humans get so possessive. And we think way too much.

So how do we survive their old age? Well, keep breathing, obviously. Some days you will have to concentrate to do it. Let the pain wash over you. Don't fight it, feel it equal not quite equal to your love. Let your tears free. Cry without judgment; it's just a different kind of breathing. But whatever else, keep moving your feet forward, just one foot in front of the other, slow and steady. Let your love for them push you forward.

And then, if all else fails, maybe a puppy.

A VERY THIN LINE

A client and I went to see a horse this week. He had belonged to her in the past, but I had known him through four owners; each time he was given up reluctantly. The gelding was ten years old; an elegant, athletic horse, smart and honest. And a sensitive horse. In other words, a wonderful horse. In other words, a horse not just anyone can ride.

He was donated to a riding program. They had lots of older horses that gave kids a good safe start, but the program also had young riders wanting to compete, and in need of a different sort of horse. Enter our gelding, elite by their standards, healthy, strong, and solid in training. The program had a dressage trainer to help, and it was a perfect match. There were grateful, happy emails exchanged, everyone cheered. Success.

Then the young rider graduated and went to college and our gelding got left behind.

Change happened and the next year there was no longer a young rider dressage program there. The economy was hitting the entire riding program extra hard. This gelding, who had been a wonderful asset, had somehow become a liability and he had to go *now*. He isn't the first good worker to get laid off in a hard economy. My client had first right of refusal, so we went to see him. It was a farewell visit; the circumstances that forced my client to part with this horse still existed and she knew she couldn't bring him home.

When we got to the barn, we met the kind rider who had

been working with him. She was new to the program and hadn't known him before. As she walked us to his pen, the rider told us that it had been a slow process; he was very nervous and much too dangerous for other riders. What?

As we get near, our gelding recognized us. It was obvious; there was an undeniable look on his face. His eyes didn't blink, he stood stock still. And we recognized him just as clearly, but the shiny, well-muscled horse we knew was skin and bones now, his back seemed to have dropped, his hooves are horribly overgrown and uneven. And yes, absolutely no doubt that he knew us.

Our gelding was nervous as the kind rider tacked him up. In the arena, he jigged a bit for her mounting, and walked off tense. After a few steps, he reared up. Twice. She says that it's unusual; that he hasn't reared in a couple of months. The rider cares and is doing her very best for him. We're shell-shocked. Our horses never rear.

We thank her and ask if we can work with him for a moment. My client began asking him for movement in their own special way of communicating; groundwork in a dialect that was all theirs. The gelding had forgotten nothing; his responsiveness gave them both confidence. When my client eventually climbed on, it wasn't immediate, but he slowly came round and soft, just barely breathing. He blew cautiously. How long had he been holding his breath?

There is such a thin line between a wonderful, well-owned and loved horse and a rescue horse. This is how it happens: A horse might misbehave, out of pain or loss, and he might get unstuck in his job. Change is hard, things fall apart. Even if people do their very best for him, cues might not mesh. It can feel like abandonment. Once he lost confidence he became undependable. A few months of maintenance costs later and the bad options started to look good.

In our case, this good gelding lost his identity because no one knew the right questions to ask him. Eventually he didn't remember who he was either. Then he was in free fall, and he knew enough to not feel safe. In the end, good horsemanship always means not blaming the horse. Our gelding did nothing wrong.

How did he go from the program's elite horse to this sad place? There were contradicting stories, defensive moments, hurt feelings, all stirred up with the passion that we all feel for horses. Does any of that matter? In the perfect world, things would look much rosier than this, but the perfect world is not visible from here.

My client and I left him there, and drove home in a car packed with dark emotions. We plotted the *what if* of our situation, of his situation. We are not naïve horse owners. Two days later we drove back up and brought him home.

It's bittersweet. Please don't go all hearts and flowers on us. Long term for this horse is uncertain. This is what we know for sure: We can give him the care he needs right now. We can remind him who he is.

LEAD MARE MUSICAL CHAIR

I'm lucky to have a herd of horses under my care. Some people call it horse poor, but I feel rich. I'm lucky to be able to keep them as a family/herd, three of them literally related, in a large pen where they can interact freely. My herd is all ages and sexes, with a wide and extreme range of personalities, and they share a resistance to change. The cherry on top is Edgar Rice Burro.

Herd dynamics is the reality show worth watching. It's at least as spellbinding as a history of the English Monarchy on Masterpiece Theater, especially if you add in the llamas and the goats.

There are galloping games of speed and daring, and mutual grooming sessions for those hard to reach places, and sometimes unrequited love affairs between different species. There is the sweetness of old age and the exuberance of youth. Long hours are spent in comfort and peace. My lead mare is not bossy or aggressive. She earns the respect of the herd with her quiet confidence; she can calm a sibling rivalry with the flick of an ear. When the games are over, there is a glow of safety and deep loyalty in the herd. You can see it when they all nap together with just inches between them.

Two months ago, we lost Windy, our lead mare. It wasn't tragic, it happened with her consent and in the right time. She was a quiet, elder mare, usually in the background; she led the herd with a peaceful confidence that almost appeared passive at first glance.

Windy's passing dropped us hollow and lost. We could barely find our way from one day to the next. Only then did I realize all that she did for us. There was a hole in the middle of the herd and no one went near the edge.

My young mare, Clara, took the passing of her mother the hardest. She was wild and worried, lost and searching. Nothing looked the same to her after. Her insecurity made her a bit aggressive; she lost her balance. The Grandfather Horse mourned deeply; he and Windy had been standing cheek to hip for years. He forgot to eat. His eyes were dead. No one ran, no one showed off. Each member of the herd reacted individually; even Edgar Rice Burro's bray was blue.

Two months later, emotions are finally leveling out and the herd was beginning to share late morning naps again. No one has stepped up to take Windy's job. Clara doesn't have the maturity and Grace is too much of a worrier. The Grandfather Horse inspired the same deference that he did before, but his heart wasn't in it. The geldings… well, they're geldings.

I have known some alpha mares that rule with aggression and intimidation, building themselves up by dominating others down. It's a leadership model based in fear and insecurity, and certainly not limited to horse herds.

Windy thought a good leader doesn't show fear or aggression. It's an art to be inspiring and not over-powering.

Windy came here from a desperate herd dispersal as a mid-life, un-rideable broodmare. But she was family, the dam of my young gelding. Windy paid me back by nurturing my herd with the tough-love sweetness of a broodmare. Under her watchful eye, the herd was calm, affectionate, and peaceful. Windy inspired mutual respect, we all felt better about ourselves having her around.

When I'm schooling my training techniques and preparing for my work with horses and riders, I like to re-read the masters that I try to emulate, like Klimke and Olivera, and added to that list, The Wild Texas Wind (our Windy).

WALTER, WALTER, WALTER

Walter is starting to settle in with us. Now I get to go to the bathroom by myself... about once every three days. It's the kind of thing you expect from a herding dog, but being a rescue as well, Walter likes to go the extra mile.

I've had a couple of requests for an update, and although it's strange that you would rather hear about Walter than another of my long-winded sermons about the benefits of dressage, here goes. Walter came here from the Wyoming Corgi Rescue one month ago.

I have always had herding dogs, but I'm new to Corgis. They need special considerations. For instance, Corgis are short enough to fit into an empty feed bag, but too long to turn around to get out. My dachshund friend welcomed me to the "Long, Low, and Level Club" and this might be what she meant.

Walter is a little over two years old and that makes him a youngster here. During morning chores, he and Tomboy, the Briard, tear around the farm at light speed. Somehow Walter manages to out run Tomboy, covering ground with freakishly long strides for such short legs. What a hand gallop, equine world take note!

His height has some advantages, he can fit into the kitty litter boxes, and when he stands underneath Tomboy, he's totally invisible. On the low (arf!) side, in our group of dogs Walter is just about the right height to get tail-whacked in the face all the time. It makes him a little squinty-eyed.

Walter isn't one to complain, but he does not really appreciate the feline sense of humor. He does like Hero, the ancient, blind, and deaf cattle dog. Hero's a heavy sleeper, smells interesting, and sometimes allows Walter on the couch.

As for me, I love him. Walter and I have so much in common: we both like second breakfast at mid-morning and hate being in the same room as a rug cleaner. We both wake up alarmingly early and cheerful! Given the chance, we are both avid nappers.

I do have one complaint. Initially there was a serious tongue problem. Although his spit was working really well as hair product, I felt there was a legitimate concern about dehydration. The licking had to stop, so I'm teaching him to hug instead. It's a tradition among Blake dogs.

Walter still quacks and yodels all day long, usually in response to the Dude Rancher, who now quacks and yodels all day as well. I guess being bi-lingual is good and Walter does have a need to be heard.

Last week I went to the Denver Dog Show and saw some of Walter's relatives. He doesn't look like them. His back is too long and lean, his legs aren't straight. I don't expect that Walter came from a very ethical breeder. It isn't a surprise. This is where I say rescue dogs are a wonderful choice, but if you do buy from a breeder, be careful. Puppy mills wear excellent disguises these days and it's easy to be tricked.

Walter still worries some. Will he be moving again? A few too many times a day, Walter gently puts his feet on my lap, and looks me square in the eye. I close my knees on either side to steady him and he leans his head rakishly to the side and gives me a big smile. Corgi lips curl at the corners and he flashes every tooth in his mouth. Walter's trying hard to look both adorable and irresistible. But as his nose rises, gravity pulls his ears back, which tightens the skin on his forehead to reveal the white of his eye. He gets that slightly alarmed and dazed look seen on women who've had too much plastic surgery.

Relax, Walter. You don't have to try so hard. You're home.

SHARING HORSES WITH LITTLE SISTERS

Ah, spring! When a young girl's thoughts turn to… horses, of course. Just like old girl's thoughts do and just the way it happens every other day of the year. Horse-crazy girls are a consistent bunch. Most of my clients are adults but now and then, I get a young rider and I love being reminded of how it all felt.

I arrived at my client's barn at the appointed hour. She met me at the arena holding Boots, her perfect mustang, but there was no sign of a kid until a second later a little girl came running, her mom and siblings following behind. It was Paris, and she'd been dreaming of this day. She wore jeans that were getting short, but all the better to see her pink cowboy boots. There was a purple helmet on top. She might have had it on all day.

Paris did some dog sitting for my client. They're neighbors and Mom helps a little. But Paris does the work and Paris gets the pay.

Paris is paid in riding lessons. I wonder what the exchange rate is in dollars, dog sitting to riding? Value wise, Paris thinks she makes a gazillion dollars a day because every minute riding is a fortune. But watching my client smiling at her wonderful mustang taking care of his young rider, she might be getting the best of the trade.

Was there someone who opened a barn door for you when you were small? Have you rescued a horse-crazy girl lately?

Paris just turned seven and she is tiny. Boots loves her, of course. At first I couldn't hear Paris; maybe she was shy or just smiling too loudly.

A few lessons later Paris told me that she had two dreams about Boots that week. (More consecutive words that she had ever said to me.) In the first dream Boots had moved away. I asked if it was a nightmare, and she nodded, showing a relieved grin—minus her front teeth. I'm hooked. In the second dream, she was riding Boots in the kitchen. Not hard to decipher this dream.

We laughed and she mounted up, stretched her heels down, and picked up her reins correctly. Then in a tiny but bold voice, "Walk on." I asked if she ever pretended to ride between lessons. "Yes, Miss Anna." It was obvious she logged mental saddle time between her lessons. It works; adults should try it.

Paris answered all questions with the words yes or good. Last week, I asked her to use a different word to describe her ride. With only a short pause, she replied, "Excellent?" Anytime a young girl refers to herself (and her horse) as excellent is a good day for all of us.

When other riders come into the arena they are deferential. We have a lunge line and a kind horse; everyone recognizes the moment. Some of us were younger than Paris and some much older, but we all remember.

At the end of the ride, Paris thanks Boots and everyone else, more than once. I can't guess the exchange rate for this either but *I'm* ready to pay someone.

Horses enrich us in more ways than we are aware. Sometimes I worry that the day will come when horses are even less available. Urban population grows and no one needs reminding how expensive horses are, but I'd hate to see the distance between horses and horse-crazy girls be any greater than it is already. They need each other.

I have a photo of the two of them. It's taken from the front; Boots is looking straight into the camera with soft eyes and just up between his ears is Paris' face, a lock of stray hair across one eye and a toothless grin as big as a horse's heart. Synergy is when the sum of the whole is greater than the parts. It's the word I think of remembering Paris and Boots. The two of seem bigger than life, but it's even more than that. It took a village to get Paris in the saddle, and yet, I think we all feel increased somehow.

Do you have a horse to share? Is there a little sister who stares at your boots with a wish too dear to ask? Do you have a favor to pay forward, from a woman long ago?

God bless generous horse-women who take the time to bring girls to the barn. Carrying them with us is a proud legacy. We learned it from our horses.

ONESIE WEATHER

Right now, it's eight degrees. Weather has been in the single digits for days here on the flat, windy, treeless prairie of Colorado. I'm absolutely giddy. Having this much cold behind us before the holidays must surely be the sign of an early spring. It's just two weeks till Solstice, longer days are on the way. Buck up, everybody! Let's talk fashion!

Is it a coverall or an overall? Another year has gone by and still, no one asks me for beauty tips. I know, having the gift of gab about horses is a wildly attractive trait for any woman, but don't sell my fashion sense short. I may not have been born in a barn, but I was born in the small shed-like house next to the barn, and that should almost count. Besides, who else is there? It isn't like Vogue or Cosmo even cares about us.

Overalls are like winter Onesies for adults, and coveralls are the ones with suspenders. It's easy to get confused. I remember years ago, getting my first adult Onesies in that rich sophisticated, yet understated, tan color. I looked in the mirror with such a thrill. My legs looked extremely long, even statuesque. If I pulled the collar up, my beauty was nearly blinding. I suppose it's possible that these arctic temperatures could freeze enough brain cells to cause some sort of reverse-anorexia. Whatever the cause, I have a nearly irrational fear of looking too thin in Carhartts this time of year.

But I had a problem. After years of slipping on frozen urine in the pens, and my Onesie being so stiff that I couldn't stand up without the help of a goat, I have recently opted for a layered approach. Long johns, of course, are the bottom layer of choice, for six months of the year at least, and then winter breeches or lined jeans, with sweatpants over top of all of them. The most layers win. It fluffs out my hips and gives me that soft-seated look that geldings prefer. If I layer just as well under my barn coat, I have the festive appearance of one of those blow-up lawn ornaments so popular this time of year.

Not to mention, these layers are comfy inside, too. It's chilly in the house, even if we do have a few more heating vents than we have cats. You must sit straight in crunchy Carhartts, but with all these layers, I can slouch a bit and pull my head in, like a turtle. Warm enough to nap anywhere.

Now for accessories: I like the maximum-coverage hat approach. Still, I find the camo face covers with the little nose tent a bit oppressive, just like those chic black knit hats that roll down over your face and make you look like a terrorist or an ATV enthusiast. I like to go old school with a nice homey (and homely, now that I think) Elmer Fudd hat with the flaps down. Sure, I get mistaken for Andy Griffith from time to time, but it's worth it for the good will. Caution: You will be addressed as *Sir* from time to time.

Since Manolo Blahnik doesn't have muck boots in his fall collection, I go with the original army green, big-toed, pull-on variety. These boots are elegant enough to be considered distant cousins of Crocs. Yes, that good. Hummer-like on slick ground, and big enough for a nice pair of wool socks, these boots are the choice of barn goddesses everywhere. Yes, they do make some muck boots with floral patterns but know that it will be like wearing a big red *T* on your forehead. *T* for Tourist.

You have to ask yourself: How did an awkward tomboy of a girl, with horse hairs in her pockets, grow up and become the strong, self-possessed beauty I am now, all these years later? I follow two rules. In matters of the heart, I take my dog's advice. His answer is always yes. In all other matters, like courage, character, and beauty, I trust my horse's opinion. He's a truth detector; he isn't fooled by outward distortions or the habits of our culture.

I've been showing up in the barn looking like this for years now. No one thinks I should grow my hair long or freshen my lipstick. When you spend enough time with horses, they appreciate you for the true qualities they respect: commitment, confidence, and strength. Is there anything more beautiful that?

So, that's my beauty tip: In this lousy, miserable cold put on a few layers and go to the barn. You don't have to stay long. The horses will remind you right away that beauty is an inside job. That, and a new pair of socks, is more than enough to get you through these eight degree days.

THE OLD AGE FISCAL CLIFF

Could there be a more beautiful animal than a horse? Even old ones who lean against the barn to nap in the sun? Maybe my lifestyle has brainwashed my eye to see horse proportions as the gold standard but when I think other animals are beautiful, it's usually because they remind me of a horse.

And having said that, horses are sadly frail by design with small feet, a large body, and a delicate digestive system. Add to this that horses should graze 24/7 and mimicking that is a challenge in our populated world. Horses are a cornucopia of delight for a lonely veterinarian.

As the amount of open range has decreased, the quality of veterinary information and care has increased. That's good; we do a better job of caring for all the animals that we live with—dogs and cats too. Baseline prices for food and general vet care are costly but fairly easy to predict. It's forecasting the emergency situation that's hard.

Do we all have at least $15,000 per horse in an emergency savings account? Along with another few thousand dollars for each dog and cat? No? You don't have a trust fund for each animal? Then there's insurance. It's the obvious answer for the single horse owner, but what if you have a herd?

Okay, then let's pretend that all of us have all the money in the world for all our animals in any emergency. In other words, let's pretend it's a perfect world. Then our horses get old.

If we put aside emotions for a moment and just do the math,

older retired horses have all the usual vet work that younger horses have, plus a few chronic conditions. A pattern begins to evolve: The old horse needs a vet call and then improves with treatment, but not as good as before. Time passes and the vet is out for another old-age reason, and again the horse survives and again, not to his previous strength. He's living a slow decline. Not bad enough to euthanize, but not entirely comfortable either. If you didn't have insurance before, he's probably too old to qualify now. If you do have it, coverage usually decreases as the horse gets older.

I would spend any amount of money if it would turn back the clock and make my horse ten years old again. But instead each investment seems to leave my elders frailer, with less energy and fewer teeth. Emotions aside (as if…), old age is financially grueling and a threat to the entire farm population. Old age is my barn's fiscal cliff.

At some point, it's time for a strategic retreat. I notice it's easier to make this judgment—balancing love with technology and finances—for other people's animals rather than those in my own barn.

I grew up on a failing farm and unemotional decisions were made daily. If an animal was not pulling its weight, there was an easy solution and it wasn't calling the vet. It was as brutal as it was natural. My Dad would think he raised an idiot if he was alive to know that I was feeding a geriatric community during a drought.

I can't anthropomorphize my horse's age, but he does not make retirement look appealing. I know in the wild, nature would have taken him years ago. Has science circumvented nature? Have I turned him into a science project? When did the natural process of aging become a war to fight with science and money?

It's complicated pondering these weighty questions of budget, fiscal cliffs, and the nature of being. I just want a work-able budget, with quality of life and health care for my elderly. And a good night prayer for all of us.

WHY WE NEED HORSE FRIENDS

"You know, no one will ever care about your horse the way that you do." My friend said it in a testy voice. I'd gotten my first horse since leaving home and she'd heard about nothing but him for the last month. Her support was wearing thin. She missed her friend who cared about art and music and movies.

A few months later, a different friend returned home to introduce her new baby. It was her dream come true, and she was so in love with her little girl that it was hard to get a word in edgewise. She didn't ask about my colt and I didn't bring him up. But when I was visiting, holding the baby while she showed me photos (of the same baby), she asked, "What time do you have to go to the barn?" I smiled and reminded her, "I *get* to go to the barn."

I needed some horse friends fast before I alienated everyone I knew.

Then one day a woman walked into my goldsmith gallery. I was soldering in my studio in back, and I told her I would be right out. She walked back to my studio door and glanced to the right at the photos on the wall. "Is this your horse?" She invited me to her barn to meet her horses, and a friendship began. Many years later, the day after I lost a very special gelding, I saw her name on my caller ID. It was years since we boarded together, but she was a horse friend, she knew. I choked out a meager hello, one word more than she got out. There was a brief silence on the other end, then tears before words. I'm proud to say Susan is still my friend, and I'm blessed with other horse friends just like her.

Friends who agree with Ralph Waldo Emerson, *"Riding a horse is not a gentle hobby, to be picked up and laid down like a game of solitaire. It is a grand passion. It seizes a person whole and once it has done so, he/she will have to accept that his life will be radically changed."*

The Dude Rancher says the same thing differently, *"They walk among us, they look just like anybody else but they're NOT."* He's right (even if he means it another way.)

Does this ever happen to you? You read some horrific story about horse abuse, or you have a neighbor whose daily neglect wears on your heart, or maybe someone at your barn is really hard on their horse. In that moment, the hurt and anger at your own species can result in an I-hate-everybody mood.

I was in that mood three weeks ago. A client and I had gone to see a horse she had previously owned, and I had trained. I wrote about him and the *Very Thin Line* between a well-loved and owned horse and a rescue horse, as a way of trying to get past the hard feelings in that transition of bringing this sweet gelding back home.

I am truly humbled, overwhelmed, and so grateful for the out-pouring of support from so many friends. There were lots of similar stories and such good will shared, for crying out loud, some of them even offered to send money to help! My heart swells with pride in all of you—my horse friend/strangers—a simple thank you doesn't convey my gratitude at all.

Some of you asked for updates (like worrying about your own horses isn't enough!) Our gelding is good. His eye is soft again and Edgar Rice Burro is keeping him company. His badly overgrown hooves are trimmed. He has a saddle mark on his back that is deeply indented but he gets a massage this week, and with correct work those muscles will return.

I'm not sure who I was trying to protect by not using his real name but it's Namaste. Do you know the word? It is a Buddhist/

Hindu salutation, translated to mean my spirit honors yours or the Divine spark in me bows to the Divine spark in you. It's a great name for a horse, isn't it?

It's a bit woo-woo for barn girls maybe, but Namaste should be how horse friends greet each other. It's what I mean when I say howdy. (And thanks, I've got your back, too.)

RELATIONSHIP STATUS: IT'S COMPLICATED

I've been thinking about the words we use to label our relationship with the animals in our lives. It isn't politically correct to say we own a horse; instead, we are its caretaker. That dog doesn't belong to you, you're its guardian. Swell.

Referring to an animal as a family member is the norm; it's common to hear someone in the barn refer to themselves as Big Red's Mom, or say that Bandit is their fur-child. No shortage of Fur-Daddies either. I understand the intention and if the words fit, go with it. It won't be the last time your real kids roll their eyes at you, even if they love their little brother, Rowdy. If you don't have actual kids, it will make people think that you dress the fur-babies up in little pink dresses and sit them at the dinner table with you. Anything that makes people look at us squinty-eyed is good.

For me, the mom/child terminology doesn't fit. I'm not Clara's Mom. I knew her Mom and she was pretty special. I wouldn't pretend to sit in that throne. Edgar Rice Burro, being bigger in legend than life, is no one's fur-baby. And my Grandfather Horse, twenty-six years old today, is certainly deserving of all the dignity shown an elder statesman. After all he has taught me, maybe I should be his Skin-Baby. But that's just gross.

I think it's an amazing thing to be a horse or dog, there is so much to envy about them. Are we sure that being their species isn't preferable to being human? Don't we aspire to the position of Lead Mare?

"Man is a wingless animal with two feet and flat nails." —Plato.

It doesn't sound so great when you put it like that.

How do I describe this relationship? Significant other? That always sounds like an oxymoron to me, and BFF is a little too pink. Let me check the list of options on Facebook…

In an open relationship? Humans might frown on a communal lifestyle, but herds like it. Besides, being a singleton and standing alone in the light of my love is blinding. They are only too happy to share me. "Look, she got another horse. Thank God."

Married? As in "Till death do us part?" Of course, but does that make me a polygamist as well? Divorced? From animals? I can't imagine it. Widowed? Three times so far this year.

A civil union has the sound of workman-like training, but seems to lack both rudeness and brilliance. If you spend more time in the barn than the house, does a horse count as a domestic partnership?

What about the *It's Complicated* status? Does this one fit? My animals inform every decision I make, whether financial, real estate, or work related, to dovetail with their care and well-being—just like a good parent. I invest my passion in hopes and dreams that include them—just like a lover. I remember stories of those animals that are long passed—like ancestors kept alive through memory. It's complicated is a status with an open-ended feel, blurring traditional titles and perplexing in its scope.

Maybe the *It's Complicated* status will have to do because there is no *All of the Above* status.

WALTER KILLS (BAGS) AT LURE COURSING

Dominating athleticism... Razor sharp senses... Intense animal magnetism... Walter the Corgi!

It's been three months since Walter came here from Wyoming Dachshund and Corgi Rescue to save us from a quiet and peaceful life. We wanted to celebrate in a special way. I suggested a *Man from Snowy River* film festival, but Walter wanted more.

We settled on Lure Coursing. It was an obvious choice for a Corgi athlete like Walter. Lure Coursing is a relative of greyhound racing, but the course has corners and runs across the yucca-adorned prairie. White plastic bags hopefully take the place of a live rabbit. Runs are sometimes punctuated by tumbleweed twisters.

First, we registered with AKC. Now we can compete in all sorts of performance events like rally, agility, and herding. They asked me to pick his registered name and being a rescue dog, we weren't burdened with elite kennel names or fancy parent names. I picked a name all about him: Walter, Walter, Walter.

We arrived early and watched a run. I wasn't sure Walter would even know what to do. Then a run started and the plastic bag whizzed by on a wire with a quick dog in hot pursuit. Walter nearly collapsed my lung, trying to launch out of my arms and join the hunt. When I got my breath back, I decided we should return to base camp and save ourselves for the real thing. I didn't know how much spectating my body could take.

It was the perfect day, and Walter ran like the wind, leaving surprised onlookers cheering. Then he had second breakfast; hard-boiled duck eggs and roast chicken. Athletes like a high protein snack. He didn't want a nap, but he was willing to meditate. Then finally the second run, even faster than the first.

And just when it could not get one tiny bit better, we came back on Sunday and did it all again.

Have I mentioned how nice all the people were? And the dogs were having a spectacular time. This is an event where the dogs run with glee and bark with abandon. There is very little human intervention unless you count the cheers and congratulations for all the dogs.

Walter earned his Coursing Ability title Sunday morning, now he has letters at the end of his name. What does a title mean to us? It's a stamp on our passport; it means we shared this momentous event and I expect others. It means that even if we met under bittersweet conditions, we are a team now and we plan to travel side by side from here on out.

On Walter's last run of the weekend, he started strong and pulled like a locomotive. It was a much hotter day and the finish line was up a long hill. His time just as quick: three hundred yards in just a bit over thirty seconds. Do the math, bunnies.

We came home and went back to our weekday lives. Just when I'd convinced Walter that he could nap through my trips to the bathroom, he's fallen in love all over again and can't let me out of his sight. Guess I'm still his favorite lure.

Then yesterday, I was digging in my tote bag and a plastic bag with some fasteners from the hardware store fell out. Walter grabbed bag and ran to the far end of the house. He would have run another three hundred yards if the front door had been open. I think there is some other title for that.

My hero: Walter, Walter, Walter, C.A.: Making the prairie safe from marauding white plastic bags. I know there are some horses out there who want to thank him.

RESCUED BY A HORSE

Have you ever been rescued by a horse? It happens more often than you'd think.

I've been thinking about Julie. Cool name, isn't it? I make no apologies. I was six years old and thought it was the best name ever. I thought Angela was a good name, too.

Julie was a pinto pony. She was mean as a snake and I was pretty fearful, especially after the day she kicked me in the face. We both got in trouble for that. Sometimes during milking, my father lifted me onto her bareback and then he'd shoosh her down the dairy barn aisle. Julie was afraid of him—we all were—and she'd scurry away in a quick buck/trot gait with me hanging on to anything I could, at least for a while.

Then I'd hit the ground, where I learned my first riding rule: If you get bucked off, you climb back on. It was years and years before I found out the real reason to remount had to do with the horse. At six years old, I thought you got back on because it was better than what your dad did if you didn't.

It defies logic that in between bouts of trying to kill me, Julie saved my life. But she did. We were never great riding partners but sometimes when we hid out together, I knew she understood me. I can't explain it any better than that but she didn't need me to... horses know the human heart.

In a few years, we lost our farm and all my pets were sold at auction. Our family moved to another state, but somehow Julie was still vaguely around, just out of view. What if our first ponies become guardian angels? It would explain a lot, wouldn't it?

Do you ever try to understand this tie between horses and humans? A drug habit would be cheaper and easier to break. Horses take most of our time and all our money. They require bold courage and soft humility, simultaneously! And no matter how great our commitment is, we're always asked for more.

Yet somehow in the middle of this dysfunctional addiction, they rescue us. We all need it and they all do it. Some of us get rescued from vanity and fashion sense. Some of us get rescued from fear and loneliness, and some of us get rescued from the danger of our own species. Sometimes special horses come deep into the dark places inside of our own hearts, and carry us out to safety.

In another way, horses are born victims. They are a prey species, like rodents or deer, which are designed to be food for others. But unlike other prey, with grace and strength, they reach out and trust their predators. It's brave and crazy, the way they herd-up with us. Maybe they understand inclusiveness more than we do but it doesn't always end well. Horses frequently need rescue from unscrupulous people.

So, it's a cycle. Horses and humans take turns rescuing each other. Does that make us co-dependent? Is that a bad thing?

The more I work with horses, the more I respect them. Even in their fear, they're trying to trust. Some of them have known nothing but abuse from humans and yet they continue to try. Maybe the biggest lesson horses teach us is about forgiveness. The horse word for that is rescue.

FARM ANIMALS IN THE ZOO?

A friend and I spent the day at the zoo last week. Colorado Springs has a wonderful zoo, on the side of Cheyenne Mountain with lots of natural habitats. It's always ranked in the top ten in the country. As zoos come and go, it's a pretty special place.

The art of keeping wild animals in cages has improved over the last few decades but I still hate it. Some species tolerate it on some level but many show stress and depression. At the same time, some species would be extinct without zoos. I can debate both sides of the love/hate zoo argument. In the end, seeing the kids' awe and enthusiasm melts my cynical heart. For so many people, a zoo is the only chance they have to experience live animals. It isn't the same on video and we need more people to care about animals enough to want to protect them.

While we were there, a docent talked with us about the ways that animals end up there, and how they work with individual animals to help them assimilate. It wasn't much different than the things I do to introduce new horses to my barn. They use active enrichment programs to add to quality of experience that sound similar to my barn, too. In the giraffe pen, I saw a male weaving and tongue chewing; I know what that would mean if a horse was doing it.

To tell the truth, the work looked familiar and my farm has been called a zoo from time to time. It isn't necessarily a compliment and neither job is as romantic as it sounds. Still, mountain goats look enough like my goats, llamas and camels are cousins, and zebras are equid enough. Infinity Farm has seven species. Having a pond brings more wild animals around: birds, coyotes, deer, and antelope. Then there's Hank, the cat, who regularly brings down adult rabbits for lunch. Do you want to tell him he's domesticated?

Infinity Farm gets lots of visitors—kind of like the zoo. And we love company. Once an entire bus-load of folks from a nursing home came for a visit. The animals were thrilled that day. And of course, people do drop by to meet Edgar Rice Burro. That's expected when you live with someone of his celebrity status.

Horse-crazy girls come for lessons, and tell their Moms that they want to live in a place just like this when they grow up. (I hope they do, but I hope they have a second bathroom.) Sometimes couples come visit, and as they leave, I can almost hear the wife say, "See, Honey, it could be worse. You could be married to her." Well, if it means you can get another cat, use me as a threat. It's fine.

The season is changing again. All the signs say one more summer is over. Geese are on the pond; hawks are hunting the pasture. The mice are moving inside the house and the flies have all gone nuts. Even for flies. The horses are well on the way to growing thick winter coats. Edgar Rice Burro, more conservative than the horses, started his winter coat six weeks ago.

Between the June fire that turned us into an evac zone, and four floods in August, it's a summer I'm glad to see behind me. Fall brings the best riding weather, but I always miss the great company we get during the summer.

Noah came from urban Virginia. He has horse-crazy girl cousins who take lessons here. Afterward watching their lesson, he asked to pet Grace. I told him one of my favorite horses shared his name, and he had the good manners to smile big. Naturally I tried to suck him into doing chores with me.

We went out to bring horses in, stopping on the way for Sebastian to smell Noah's breath and to share some goat chat.

It's just good manners. Before we got the first horse in his run, I'd lost count of the times Noah said thank you. The hugs started before the second horse was in her run. Eventually his family dragged him away, but I got a thank-you card this week. A thank-you card from a teenage boy? What is this world coming to? He signed it *City Boy*. I might have called him that.

I'm not sure what the future holds. The world is a pretty complicated place for all of us species to survive together. Change happens. When I was young, I could babysit to buy enough hay to feed my horse over the winter. Now a parent practically needs a second job to keep a horse. Will the day come when horses and farms literally become zoos? In the future, will owning horses become so out of reach for mainstream folks, that horses will seem as exotic as giraffes?

THIS TOO SHALL PASS

The temperature had plummeted to seventy degrees, with a light breeze. Welcome, September. There was almost an hour of daylight left, the clouds were bubbled and layered, and the air was very sweet at my altitude.

I'm about a horse and a half tall, riding Namaste. He came here five months ago from a sad place where he had fallen between the cracks.

There's peace in his eye now, and I'm slowly asking his strength to return. He's a sensitive gelding who thinks too much, so while we walk, I keep the conversation going. He likes to talk about himself, like all good horses do. So, I ask him about his walk: big steps, lateral steps, supple and forward all together. We talk rhythm, and rib stretches, and the softest questions are about that right side of his poll. It's a perfect ride.

This too shall pass.

It's been twenty years and those words still ring in my somewhat deaf ears. I had a trainer who used to say it all the time, especially if I was in a pit of despair about whatever my current riding drama was. My horse would be confused, my hands would pull, and our frustration was nearly blinding. I was always fighting—whatever the problem was that week. It was like teen angst, only I wasn't a teenager. Awkward. And she said it again, *this too shall pass.*

It felt dismissive, but it wasn't. She just had a larger view of things. They were the same words she told me when I did something really well, only with a chuckle then. She gave success and failure the same measure, after all; they are different sides of the same coin. I learned it from her, and on this perfect evening, I need to thank her once again.

Two boarders were riding with me, both were giving soft praise, laughing, trotting lightly past us. No boom box tonight, instead the music of rhythmic hooves, blows and snorts, praise and laughter.

Is Infinity Farm such an ethereal place that all horses and riders dance like angels? Hardly, not by a mile. Both riders are on the rebound from falling in a hole. That's what I call being given an opportunity to refine one's approach to riding. It's uncomfortable but not terminal.

If there were a graph of the ups and downs of training, it would look like a heart beat on a monitor. Because ups and downs are a sure sign of life going on.

The sun eventually gets low and the breeze settles. Namaste has had more than a few bad days in his life, just being a horse living with humans. I am sure there are natural born riders out there, but I'm not one of them. Right now, we're golden. *This too shall pass*, this perfect moment, like all the other less-than-perfect moments that came before. Maybe it isn't really about good or bad, so much as making friends with this process of learning to ride.

Who ever said it was easy to climb on top of a sentient creature, a thousand pounds strong, and find partnership in a trot, or a flying change?

And as sweet as it is to have a good ride, it can be even better to have a less-than-good ride. I get a little excited for you. It isn't that you or your horse has fallen short somehow. It's an opportunity to go back to the basics, the warm home plate to begin again, because each time we return and practice basics we gain a deeper understanding of ways to help our horse, and ourselves.

"Life is difficult. This is a great truth, one of the greatest truths.

It is a great truth because once we truly see this truth, we transcend it. Once we truly know that life is difficult—once we truly understand and accept it—then life is no longer difficult. Because once it is accepted, the fact that life is difficult no longer matters." —M. Scott Peck. He wrote this about life, but riding is life for a lot of us, and it holds true.

Riding is hard. Can we all agree on this one point? A whole lot of riding is counter-intuitive. On top of that, the degree of difficulty is increased by our personal degree of desire. None of us are short on desire, are we?

Most of us are fairly clear that fighting our horse doesn't get the best work. We are always training either resistance or release, and release makes for a happy horse. Fighting ourselves is no different. The more we flog ourselves for not being perfect, the more energy is wasted heading the wrong direction. If you have evolved enough to not blame your horse, good for you. Now, give yourself a break, too. Riding is hard, and *this too shall pass.*

HOW TO TELL IF YOU'RE TURNING INTO A HORSE

"Anthropomorphize" is that huge word that's hard to pronounce. It means to attribute human characteristics to animals or inanimate objects. In other words, make animals over in our image. Is there a word for making ourselves over in theirs?

There are so many ways that I'm totally human. I walk on only two feet in the barn, mucking and feeding and doctoring. Those are human jobs. I have a book of checks that have Barn Account printed on them, and I'm pretty proud of what I pay for around here. Again, a human skill. And finally, I can pass for a human in a crowd of humans; some of them even like me.

But between working with my extended herd of horses and riders, and taking care of everyone here at Infinity Farm, the vast majority of my time is spent with horses. It impacts how I perceive things and I notice I'm taking on some horse behaviors. I'm not complaining; it isn't necessarily a bad thing.

No, I don't take a dirt bath after a ride, and other than oatmeal in the morning, I don't lust for grain. I would like to look as smooth and shiny as my horses, but nope, I never will. Let's not even mention athleticism or grace.

I did develop a deep, low heh-heh-heh sort of laugh that sounds like a nicker. Or to be more precise, a particular mare's nicker. I hadn't even realized it, until she pointed it out to me. But what I'm talking about is even a bit more socially awkward than that. The behaviors I'm taking on are subtler than that; it's all happening inside my head.

One of the biggest differences between humans and horses is our senses. Being prey animals, horses have a keen awareness of their environment. Humans are blind, hairless mice in comparison. But if we spend enough time trying to understand and communicate with horses, slowly our senses improve. Balance and body awareness changes first. We need that physical awareness to learn that in order to ride. I have a hearing loss that I notice less because being with horses taught me to hear with my eyes. Over time it almost seems as if each of our senses improve, but I think as we are really becoming more present and aware in the moment.

But I digress. The situation usually happens when I'm doing some random human communicating. Everything is fine in the beginning; we're all standing around, like a bunch of mares in the shade, swishing our tails against the flies. I'm fine as long as everyone is polite and the interchange is willing. Questions are asked and I get to volunteer an answer, just like my horses. As long as things stay in a peaceful, *Classical Training* sort of tone, I'm good.

But passive coercion begins; humans are rarely honest for long. Some of us think it's okay to lie if we have good intentions, so we distort the truth or we're passive about asking for what we want. We use insinuation instead of honesty. We say one thing when we mean another, and then pass it off as a joke. I'm humorless about manipulation. I start to feel restricted, my eyes show it first. I get squinty. "Is that person actually trying to move my feet about this? No way would he/she be a decent Boss Mare." I long for clear communication; I notice I don't enjoy groundwork with humans as much as I do with horses. Initially both species can be pretty rude, but horses become peaceful partners with confidence building-groundwork. Humans seem to have more resistance.

From a position of herd dynamics, most of the leadership

I see in the human world is pretty self-serving and ego-based. They want to be Boss Mare for all the wrong reasons. Thinking about the best for the herd is rare, and too often leaders have ulterior motives. When the words feel predatory, we must use our senses to find our bearings. Does that woman have a jig to her walk? Can I see just a bit too much white around her eye? Does her body look tense? If a horse wouldn't trust her, then neither do I.

More often than not, I disengage a hip and break eye contact. I don't like confused or contradictory communication. If I get frustrated enough, I'll either blow up or shut down. Like a horse.

I prefer a herd with a kind Boss Mare; she'll be inclusive. Old geldings and young fillies all share a warm barn. They tolerate humming llamas and goats who pee where they eat, because it takes all kinds.

What happens if I keep acquiring horse behaviors this way? Maybe one day, my eyes will get big and soft and I'll know forgiveness and trust. If I spend enough time with horses, maybe I'll finally have mare eyes.

In the meantime, I'll keep fine tuning my limited senses and practice moving other humans' feet. It's all about positive leadership.

WALTER ON THE PREDATOR/PREY THING

Walter likes to think he's an only dog. Walter also likes to think of himself as amazingly athletic, incredibly fascinating, and wildly handsome with an exceptional rack of ears. Walter is not burdened with a lack of self-esteem in his own mind. Remember Walter? He is the Corgi that came here to rescue us from the church-like quiet of a moonlit prairie six months ago. Walter has some insights to share about being a semi-reluctant predator.

For sake of conversation, Walter categorizes the world in two groups. The wide-apart eyes are prey animals. Their purpose is to live a happy life and be eaten. Then there are close-together eyes, it's their purpose to live a happy life and eat others. They are predators and a bit adversarial by accident of birth.

Walter likes to think of himself as an only dog, so he considers the other dogs that live here as mere obstacles that sometimes get between him and me. Tomboy, the Briard, takes exception to his lack of respect for her masterful multi-tasking leadership of the entire farm. So Walter is careful to stay below her radar; easy to do being short.

***

I own this woman from the ankles down.

***

When Walter set about finding friends here at Infinity Farm, he decided to ignore all animals here that are significantly taller than him, so no horse friends or llama friends. He could have had a great friend in Edgar Rice Burro since they share so many opinions about politics and food, but Walter is just unwilling to look up. It makes his neck stiff. He did consider the goats briefly, being a middle size and all, but upon reflection, it didn't seem prudent because that weird angle of iris in the goat's eyes made him uncomfortable.

That only leaves cats and ducks as potential friends of a certain non-altitude. Walter likes the ducks; they march along in formation leaving little treats in their wake, and quack kind of like he does. He can herd them up and down the fence line like a drill sergeant because ducks are prey animals and don't ask many questions. It's easy being friends with wide-apart eyed animals. Still predator/prey friendships like this are clearly one-sided.

***

About face and waddle along now.

***

Walter likes to think of himself as a free-thinker, not bound by prejudice. But at the same time, he thinks cats are alien walk-ins, or devil's spawn, or worse, partying predators that have no respect for common decency. Walter just doesn't trust their intentions. They sit on high things where they're hard to see and then pounce for no good reason. They lie in doorways, blocking traffic for hours. And sometimes when they look asleep, they'll hook a claw in your ear, just for the fun of it, for crying out loud! Cat-astrophic!

Walter likes to think of himself as a vegetarian because he is fond of all kinds of non-meat food. But it isn't true. He has close-together eyes; it's only his ears that are wide-apart. I feed Walter a raw meat diet and he shows a firm commitment to meat by quacking and whining for an hour before dinner, just on the off-chance I might forget how to tell time.

***

One day it will rain bacon!

***

He may want to think of himself as a vegetarian, but the hard truth is that Walter is a predator, with blood on his paws. And still the cats disrespect him. It's embarrassing.

I notice that the other dogs don't have this problem. Tomboy is an assertive barn manager that lets that orange cat sleep right on top of her. She has the self-confidence of doing her job well and knowing her place. It's good to be the Queen.

We humans like to think we're better than other animals and that we've evolved past all this, but it isn't true. We're still predators. Some of us are honest and happy with our job description, like Tomboy. Most of us are like Walter. We like to think of ourselves as not really predators at all, because it's confusing in the middle range where we flop around between living a dream of world domination, and the humiliating reality of being used as catnip. So, we humans are flip-floppers, too.

It is appealing to want to partner with a horse, whose wide-apart eyes could see us differently. But if we flounder in our predator confusion like Walter does, the friendship will be as one-sided as a duck's.

THE BATTLE CRY OF AN OLD GRAY MARE

"Do you work out?" I find this question difficult to answer. I'm never sure what they're asking but it was even worse when I was single. I thought might be a code phrase for some other question.

I do practice Yin Yoga. That's where you tie yourself up in a knot and breathe for a while. I don't think that qualifies as working out really, but I smile all the way home.

But if you're asking do I go to a mirrored room and lift weights, not because they need to be somewhere else, but just to put them back down in the same spot? Do I run laps of something, even if no one is chasing me? Do I dancercise to music that makes my head want to explode? No.

I don't work out; I train horses and riders. It's outdoor work so I have an unwanted tan in the middle of winter. Sunscreen doesn't work nearly as long as I do. I wear out boots regularly and I think they shouldn't wear out so fast. Recently I got a new smart phone that has a footstep counting app. It seems I'm in the extremely active footstep category. Hardly a surprise. I notice knowing how many steps I take makes my feet a little more consciously sore, and maybe those boots actually were well made. For someone with a desk job.

I don't work out; I do chores. Infinity Farm has a decent sized herd and I'm that odd sort who loves mucking. Each week

I haul off around a ton of manure. Literally. I muck it into tubs, lift the tubs to dump the muck into the trailer, and then off-load the trailer at the recycler. By doing this, I save enough money each month to feed one of my retired rescue horses and I think it strengthens my "retirement" plan as well. But that adds up to two tons of lifting a week; it would be gratuitous to add in the hay and feed I carry. But no, I don't lift weights.

A while back, my monthly load of hay was delivered by a couple of new guys. They were twenty-ish and had spent a little too much time cowboy dressing, if you know what I mean. They were bragging about riding bulls. (Just for the record, I'm not a fan of bull riding. I think it's silly.) They were clearly trying to show off and it baffled me. It seemed almost flirtatious the way they carried on. It made my head tilt like a Corgi. Let's be clear, I'm too old to be their mother. Or maybe they were flirting with each other? I don't understand men.

As they stacked the hay in my barn, I off-loaded thirty bales to the back of my truck to take to another spot. When I got back from stacking my load, they were still chipping away at their sixty bales, doing more talking than tossing hay.

I was thinking of telling them that they throw (hay) like a girl, but they aren't that good, and I know how fragile baby bull riders can be.

It's an old insult, to tell a man that he throws like a girl, but the insult never made any sense to me. I had a high school P.E. teacher who retired from fast-pitch softball and threw me a few balls to show the class. Fast-pitch is an understatement. And Serena Williams plays tennis like a girl, doesn't she? I think the original meaning is lost and now might be the time to really take some pride in it. Are you that strong?

No bragging, I know I'm not out of the ordinary for my lifestyle. I have a lot of women friends who throw even more like a girl than me. But I'm doubly dangerous; I'm no longer a demographic now that I'm on the far-side of midlife. They can't sell me cosmetics, or kitchen doodads, or a vacation home because I'm already living in it. Advertisers think I no longer exist, as does a good segment of the population. It's kind of liberating.

Beware the old gray mare: I'm not dead yet, and I throw like a girl.

AN OCTOBER ROMANCE

It was innocent. They were looking for companionship, that's all. Each had suffered a loss and they were drifting a bit, hoping to find a friend. Nobody said anything about falling in love.

Sumo came to Infinity Farm as a kid with his twin, Elvis, twelve years ago. They were always carefree and ornery goats, sleeping spoons even in the hottest weather. One day Elvis started to fail; we did our best to help him but he was gone in hours. Sumo mourned with elegance and profound sorrow. We were all humbled by the depth of emotion, as he bleated his blue heart dry. Then he began the search for a new twin. Goats are pragmatists.

Edgar Rice Burro came here from a planet with no donkeys. Can you imagine? When he got off the trailer, the two donkeys who lived here brayed at him. He was giddy with glee and reckless abandon. He had no idea! They frolicked and stayed up all night, and relished common sense and good manners. And then one day, the other donkeys were gone, and Edgar was alone again. In a barn filled with horses and llamas and goats, he brayed a melancholy moan with each exhale. Loudly. Unceasingly. Operatically. He took some consolation from the Grandfather Horse. He did his job and welcomed the visitors from the local horse rescue who came for training visits. He's been known to enjoy the company of a certain brash young filly. He adjusted his life. After all, everybody liked him. He was probably happy enough.

Sumo began his search to find a new twin in the logical place. His first choice was the One-Who-Feeds. I had my doubts. I work with a couple of dogs in my truck already. The other goat, Just Joe, wasn't a possibility. He'd lost his twin years ago, but even before that, he had forsaken his species for another, and joined the herd of llamas. Make a choice like that and there's no turning back. (Not that Joe ever wanted to.) Sumo tried hanging with the Grandfather Horse, who shared his breakfast happily, but the chemistry wasn't just right. Sumo longed for a like mind and a sideways heart—the kind goats appreciate.

It's funny, you can live in the same village and see neighbors every day, but then one day something shifts. You catch an eye in a different light, and something gives you pause. It's like recognizing someone, and even though the exterior appearance is familiar, you see something brand new. It's very exciting and wild but you know you aren't a kid, or a donkling. Is it too late to take a chance?

It's an unlikely match but Sumo and Edgar have a lot in common. They both really, really like alfalfa mush. One sings just a little louder than the other, but both enjoy vocalizing; yodeling out tunes like *Stand by Your Man* and *The Yellow Rose of Texas*. If I hadn't been singing harmony, I would have gotten audio. And when it's all said and done, on the most primal level they find each other's statuesque ears very attractive.

Being older and somewhat wiser, they each had low expectations from romance. There are no frantic public displays of passion and drama. It's more like watching moon-rise from a cozy stall. They nap together and share hay. Sometimes if you squint your eyes just right, they look like a very attractive older couple. Like they've been together forever.

Inter-species relationships are always critically scrutinized. Of course, there were naysayers. Some say that goat only wants a bigger donkey-sized piece of shade to sleep under. Others say that donkey only wants to steal Sumo's hay. Some were jealous of the comfort; some just don't like change of any kind. Not everyone wished them well.

Sumo and Edgar think it's worth weathering the resistance. On cool fall days, it's nice to have someone to scratch, someone to lean on, and someone to watch the change of season with.

"Shared joy is a double joy; shared sorrow is half a sorrow." —Swedish Proverb

It's a simple life on the farm. Time passes and sharp edges are eventually burnished to a dull glow. Even flying in the face of convention becomes an ordinary occurrence. Maybe in the end, all any of us want is acceptance. The rest is all apples and carrots.

NO SMALL FEET. I MEAN FEAT

His name was Archie. He got introduced to me by that name, but I prefer being a bit more formal with him, as a sign of respect. Archibald sounds more suitable.

When I arrived at the pen he was passing time with a couple of boys in my herd, but I distracted him with a compliment and now he's on his way over for a scratch. This is *no small feat*. I have a ton of respect for this horse. It's horses like Archibald who embody the finest traits we love about equines.

I'm fostering him here for a local horse rescue. Archibald had the kind of start that isn't unusual for a rescue horse. Neglect. There is a long list of ugly details about his herd—he was living in a junkyard with little hay and no water. The owners lived thirty miles away. Imagine the worst, and whatever your mind is picturing, it isn't bad enough. He was one year old, forty inches tall, and a "miniature" horse. It's a stupid breed name, miniature. They are more horse per square inch than a draft horse.

Humans have to show at least some tiny bit of respect to horses that weigh five times what they do, for reasons of self-preservation if nothing else. But not so much with a horse like Archibald. Shorter horses frequently feel the brunt of ugly manhandling. Or maybe it just hurts their pride more.

This rescued herd had little human interaction, and what they did have was brutal. Some idiots think it's easier to intimidate than to train. Rope him, slam him against a fence panel, and if that doesn't work, his feet don't get trimmed. Archibald's feet didn't get trimmed but it's hard to tell if he was especially difficult, being a young stud and all. The rest of the herd had long hooves, too.

Of course, there was no way to halter him at first. To say he was shy is an understatement; his fear was so violent that opening a stall gate would cue him to throw his body into a fence to get away. His behavior was more like a mustang's than a domestic breed. We spent hours working on our knees so we wouldn't be taller, trying to win his trust. Hours into weeks, using a slow approach to halter without violence. Eventually, with patience and good horsemanship, Archibald began to trust again.

This is what I respect the most: Archibald has such resilience, such a strong sense of self that he found a way to lay down his dark memories. It makes my heart swell with awe. He's the one creating the possibility of a better future for himself; not us. *No small feat* again.

So, he's here with me to learn to drive, but after we're done working he follows me while I muck. He's even starting to come when I call. His heart is open and welcoming. I'm not sure I would be that forgiving. Who knows why horses, especially rescues, are willing to reach out and volunteer with humans, but they do. Is there a more glorious creature than a horse?

Please think of Archibald as a complete horse, just like Percherons and Arabians, requiring no more or less. Talented but short. I refuse to use their common name, when there is really nothing *mini* about him at all. (Okay, maybe his bill for hay.)

Make no mistake, he isn't a toy for a child, just ask my herd. They defer to him with respect. He is bold and smart. Archibald is curious and courageous, and ready to partner in work with a good human.

What is a non-rideable horse good for? Everything. They excel at therapy and service work. They're brave agility horses and Archibald will pull a cart, once he has matured. Trail drive anyone? An obstacle course perhaps? It's wild fun. And naturally, he can do dressage. There are driven dressage tests and more than that, he could be trained up the levels. In-hand work was the classical approach to training in the first place. Are your horsemanship skills up to the task with a horse of this stature? He's a great teacher of those skills, if you see him in the full light of his potential.

Bold, smart, and very trainable, there is really nothing "miniature" about Archibald and his breed at all. It's just our attitude, our understanding, that's under-sized.

CREAKY OLD HORSES AND THE WOMEN WHO LOVE THEM

I have a Grandfather Horse. People say he looks good for his age. I notice the "for his age" disclaimer is probably true for me, too.

He has his very own veal pen at night; a private place he can enjoy his special mush, chew hay and spit it back out, and stay warm. Last week, I found him with his sheath terribly swollen, and surrounded a large area of edema. His run was dry, with no recent urine. OH NO. This is it; this is the end. Gasp!

Two years ago, a veterinarian told me that if gray geldings live long enough, they all end up with a tumor in their sheath area, and I've known a couple with that ailment myself. It was a death sentence; I couldn't breathe.

Disclaimer: I am a decent amateur veterinarian myself; fearless about blood or injury, I give shots easily, and I can keep a colic horse on his feet until the real vet gets there. I'm strong and dependable in an emergency. It's different with the Grandfather Horse. I notice I get a little teary when he gets his teeth checked, and sometimes my voice cracks when I say his name. What a ninny.

So, we had our first emergency vet call of the icy, miserable season. It's a tradition with the Grandfather Horse to take the change of season hard. At his age, any vet visit might be his last. The office asked if I needed a same day appointment, or if tomorrow was soon enough. I don't know, I don't have advance-hindsight. If I knew how it was going to turn out, I would know how soon I needed them. The situation looked serious enough, so I asked for same day and doubled my farm call.

The newest, youngest vet in the practice arrived. She's three years older than the Grandfather Horse. I had the horrible fear that I was going tell her maudlin stories about him. I could feel my throat start to close, and at times like this, I even make myself tired. I am an equine professional, for crying out loud! Horses are my business, and I give sage advice to other people acting like ninnies about their horses. And then my voice cracks again. After all these years, the Grandfather Horse still enjoys my embarrassment. He's likes to have an unfailingly sweet and pathetic look on his face while I humiliate myself. It was even worse before he retired.

He clearly enjoys the sweet talk and attention from the vet tech and vet, not to mention the happy injection. The check goes slowly, it's swollen and totally raw on the inside. There is an external rash that bleeds when irritated. The vet checks everything thoroughly, cleans the area, and finds no palpable tumor.

Okay, it ends up that it was *an emergency sheath cleaning*. I'm just going to pause here and wait for the laughter and jeering to die down. I deserve it. Thank you.

It's pretty predictable at this point. He stands all day on bowed legs and an arthritic hip, resting his eyes. He stands just the same way in turnout. The only exercise he actually takes is walking back and forth from his stall, and then we both take baby steps. It's the reason an old horse's sheath ends up in this disgusting smegma situation—he barely moves. He does not even feign awkwardness or apology.

It occurs to me as I'm writing that the non-horse owners might be recoiling in disgust, reading about this topic. We horse folks are fine with it. We constantly redefine polite conversation. Or maybe we just don't care.

The vet left us with meds and directions to cold hose him a few times a day, followed by an application of an aloe vera vet salve. This salve is the best part for the Grandfather Horse; he plans a very slow recovery. It's okay, my reputation with this horse is shot anyway.

The vet also added one more ailment to his chronic list. Now he has a moderate heart murmur. Oddly, I don't panic at this. After all, he has a tumor on his colon, the most likely the cause of three years of incurable diarrhea, and so much arthritis that from some angles, he has a decidedly bovine appearance. His eyesight is bad and he gets disoriented. Old age is not for the vain, and someday this list will defeat him. But not today.

I've never been even remotely passive about this horse. I remember the first time it occurred to me that he would eventually die. I owned this wild colt all of twenty-four hours and I couldn't catch him in his twelve-by-twelve-foot stall, when the thought that he was mortal crossed my mind. I clutched my throat, in tearful fear of losing him. He was seven months old.

I don't know, maybe I could find other women like me and start a support group. But I hear the first step is admitting you have a problem. I don't see any of us doing that.

WHAT HORSES WANT FOR CHRISTMAS

My mail box is full of holiday sale ads from every tack store on the planet, written by a stranger who works in the advertising department and doesn't know my barn, telling me what my horses want for Christmas. None of us here are *that* easy to shop for.

Case in point: Patent leather dressage bridles. They might be a good idea since some dressage riders can be a little goody-goody and Type A. But not in my case. My mother made me wear tight patent leather shoes to church when I was little. I don't think I could do that to a horse. Mine aren't that *church-y*.

There are new winter blankets that look like vintage flowered bedspreads. Do manure stains show less on a pattern? It doesn't matter; our blankets have family hand-me-down karma, worn by the last generation of good Infinity Farm horses, except for the Grandfather Horse who still wears the winter blanket custom made for him twenty-five years ago. It's patched and faded, but broken in just the way he likes it. When he has no more use for it, I'll put it on another horse. I'm pretty sure it has healing qualities.

But you actually know that horses don't care about this kind of stuff, right? They care about you; they care about relationship.

It's more likely that the holiday lists that they would make would include things you can't buy in a store. The usual equine requests include, "Could you help my rider get that cinder block out of her pants and loosen up some in the saddle?" Or "Please, let my rider breathe a little deeper, she's squishing my ribs." But the number one request is always the same: "Dear Santa, please bring my rider better hands." If they sold those at Dover, we'd all charter a bus and go today!

Is anything harder to learn than soft, connected contact? If we ride with our bodies; with seat and legs doing the cuing, then I like to think *we use the reins to listen to our horse*. Reins and bits should never be used for correction, just for suggestion. We humans have definitely gotten hard in the mouth about bits. Too many of us are not aware of how much we pull on the reins; stiff elbows create stiff horses. No horse will ever be happy as long as his rider has a death grip on the reins. We need to develop soft, breathing hands, steady in contact, yet fluid with the horse. Generous hands.

"It is always better to risk losing the contact a little, than to not yield at all." —Nuno Oliveira

If you want your horse happier, maybe the best gift for your horse this holiday is an investment in your skill. A little coaching from the ground might help you *hear* better with your hands. I think riding is one of those things that's pretty difficult to learn from a book, and videos aren't much better. And like most relationships, communication can always improve.

Back to shopping; it's true that when it comes to spending money there's nothing I enjoy more than shopping for my horses. But we have hay enough and blessings past all reason. Even Clara, the young mare, sees no need to gild the lily. We should all have her confidence. If anything, I would buy what we have for other horses.

Today, I was returning a couple of horses who were here for training back to the local horse rescue, and she told me they're getting ready to help a newly relinquished emaciated elderly horse. It's a common story: He's no longer ride-able, his family has fallen on hard times, and he needs help soon. I keep thinking about him; the wind is blowing cold tonight. And I know he is not the only elder lost in neglect. My Grandfather Horse has shelter and lots of hay. His age has some dignity to it; at least he is safe in our herd.

We've got what we need here, I think I'll spend my money at my local horse rescue. I'm not bragging, I never give as much as I wish I could. I'm just suggesting, like a kind hold on the reins… if you are dreaming of horses this holiday, use your generous hands to put a big red bow on an old campaigner, past his usefulness. Because it's never too late for him to be treated like a Christmas Pony!

FAMILY VALUES

Earlier this year a client was asking me for some backup horse care. A parent was in the hospital and she needed to go home. My client was working out the plan: Her dog wasn't welcome in any of her sibling's homes, so she was searching for a motel with pet options. Added to the stress, her older brother was mad that she worried for her elderly cat, mad that the dog had to come, and just plain mad, in a bossy older brother sort of way. Did I mention that my client was in her sixties? Shouldn't there be some sort of age-out limit for sibling bullying about pets? Do you still get in trouble for spending too much animal time?

Some of us were born into loving families with big hearts and open arms. Good for you, really wonderful luck.

I was raised by people who didn't want any kids or animals in their house. They reluctantly let their children come in, but never a cat or dog. Okay, there was an exception for a Chihuahua once, but he didn't live in the house so much as inside someone's shirt.

By the time we kids were gone, so were the pets. My siblings both did the perfectly respectable thing: They married, had kids, and didn't let pets in the house. My alternative lifestyle was a huge embarrassment. Was it drugs? Cult membership? Sexual orientation? No, sadly I was something even worse: A childless woman who let animals in the house, for which I received wild disapproval. If I'd had five kids in dirty diapers smoking crack, there would have been less criticism than I got for a golden retriever and a couple of cats. I stopped coming home for the holidays. (I learned it from dogs; they won't come to you if you're angry either.)

By the time I hit my thirties, my fur family had grown. Ridicule works like that sometimes. I had more dogs and cats, and worst of all, horses. They hated the horses. The bullying was endless. One year, I agreed to come to a holiday dinner at a sibling's home, knowing that my dogs weren't welcome. I got up early and took my dogs to the park and then made a quick barn visit. After my tasks were done, I drove an hour, arriving at the agreed time for dinner. The kids were lit up with post-present hysteria and the parents exhausted and depressed with the effort of the extravaganza. I got scolded for being "late." The meal came with a double helping of judgment and disapproval smacked down on my plate. By late afternoon I was getting ready to leave, but they had assumed I would sleep over. When I reminded them of the dogs at home, they seemed surprised and disappointed. With one more scolding, I thanked them and limped on home to a standing (jumping, wiggling, and licking) ovation.

By my forties, my parents had given up talking sense into me and it was widely acknowledged that my dogs behaved better than most of the relatives. My parents passed before the goats and llamas came. Not to mention the other five horses and Edgar Rice Burro.

Now I'm at the end of my fifties. My birth family is all in the wind, one way or another, along with the bullying. I've acquired a wonderful circle of friends. We cancel plans if a horse looks a bit off or a dog is sick. We beg off invitations because of agility matches or horse events. We celebrate when someone expands their family with a new dog, and add our tears to theirs when a good horse passes. Social events take place after chores. When someone excuses themselves to go home to feed, it's never an excuse to leave early, just a happy affirmation of the lives we share.

This year has been a rough year with too much adversity.

Some of us lost loved ones. Some of us feel excluded or judged unfairly or are just licking our wounds from a hard-fought battle. If you feel sometimes that the world is short on human kindness, or that your own species has let you down, I understand.

There's a Norwegian folktale that says at precisely midnight on Christmas Eve all animals can talk. That's crazy-stupid, of course. We know they talk constantly, if you care to listen. During my late-night barn walk-through on Christmas Eve, I was thinking of writing my version of this story. Peace on Earth began in a stable after all. Then I lost my train of thought while scratching noses. Out of the corner of my eye, I thought I saw the two dear dogs I lost this year, and was that the old mare standing in the shadows? I remembered generations of dogs and cats and horses who showered me with love and acceptance and blessed my life.

It's a privilege to love and care for animals every hour of every day. And especially on holidays.

RESCUE INSPIRATION

Some rescue groups prove their point by showing graphic photos of the very worst cases of abuse and neglect. These horrific images cower in a dark corner of my brain forever. Their torture leaves a mark on us, too. Maybe people think that the more blood-dried wounds, protruding bones and dull eyes I see, the more I will care. It isn't possible.

I wonder how many of us get inspired by the gore, versus the number of us that just shut down. We look away because we're full to the top with pleading eyes and it just rubs salt in the wound, not that the wound was anywhere near healing in the first place.

"You can't save them all!" That's what my mother said when I was little and it still puts a lump in my throat. What a sorry excuse for inaction. What a petty reason to not even try. Our indifference is our shame; our silence is consent. But really, my name-calling rant doesn't stop abuse, or even graphic photos, does it? How can we keep our hearts open and protected at the same time?

The first thing I can tell you is that there is no happy story about how a horse gets to a rescue. Sometimes it's that skeleton horse who's been starved, some who are distrustful and frightened by physical abuse in the guise of training, and some are just dumbed down by neglect. Some get relinquished because their human is facing impossibility. The grimy, sad details vary and there isn't always a clear villain. The one thing every rescue horse has in common is that they are there through no fault of their own.

Maybe it's counter-intuitive, and call me a Polly*Anna*, but I get inspired by happy endings and new beginnings. Here is a small sampling of what I mean:

The first time I saw Mack… well, you know how thin he was. He was an abandoned elder, used up and left. We didn't know if he would last a day. Internal organs could have begun to shut down. It was touch and go, but slowly he got stronger. Eventually he was shiny and fat—the color of a burnished penny. That's when he hooked Marcy. She picked him up, her rich laugh clearing the air, and off he went to live with her beautiful mares. Does it get better than that? Yes, it does. Marcy reports that his back has benefited from chiropractic treatments. Well played, Old Man. You deserve it.

Misty is a huge success. And it isn't just her Percheron heft, it's her heart. Or maybe it's Becky's heart, sometimes it's hard to tell where one of them ends and the other begins. Becky adopted Misty when she was young and un-trained. They've worked hard to build their partnership. Becky's passion is trail riding and Misty has a secret: You can see it plain as day in the arena when she gets the dressage cue—*inside leg to outside rein.* Relaxed and forward, Misty's neck arches, there is a soft bend and her shoulders lift. Even in that well-oiled Western saddle with the fluorescent orange *hunter-beware* cantle pack, her secret is hard to hide. Misty likes to dance.

Pipi was here with me for a couple of months. She's a mini-mule with a past. She lost her sense of humor after a few homes. She had the audacity (or honesty) to hold a grudge. She softened up some being here. Slower than slow, we negotiated getting the halter on; whatever happened to her ears, she told me, was very, very bad. You'd have to think a little left-of-normal to like Pipi. Then Julie called. She wanted a companion for her old horse… because her second horse had an inoperable tumor. Pipi would need a savvy horse person, so we asked Julie the hard questions.

She told us her ailing gelding came fourteen years before with missing teeth and a scar on his tongue. She had to go slow—he was still very head shy. We told her the truth, warning that Pipi might be the same kind of challenge. Julie nodded, "I'm good with that." I watched them together; Julie has good skills, though Pipi still doesn't believe in love at first sight. Some of us are more cautious. But she hopped in the trailer and a week later, we got photos of her grazing with her new family. Her eye was soft; I am glad she's there to help those geldings at this hard time. She has a life with their lives now.

There really is someone for everyone. That might be the most inspirational thing of all.

King (Viking) came into rescue because his owner had a bad turn of health and age; it could happen to any of us. At twenty, King had done it all. He's not retired but not sound, with some health challenges ahead. Andrea had just said goodbye to her last rescue horse at thirty-three. She knows horse care is an art. They fell in love over a shedding blade. Hard to tell who rescued who…

I got a thank you card from Andrea and King. She invited me to visit, saying, "King will always be as much your horse as he is mine."

I like that sentiment. The truth is I think all of us should feel that horses are our gift of love and responsibility. They belong to all of us. Maybe it's naïve to think we can save them all but each life has value. There's honor in the effort. And maybe we save ourselves just a bit in the process.

THE CORGI WITNESS PROTECTION PROGRAM

Did you even know there is a Corgi Witness Protection Program?

It's the one-year anniversary of the day that Walter came here from Wyoming to rescue the Dude Rancher and me from our dull and monotonous existence on the Colorado Prairie. He'd done a few things he wasn't proud of and wanted a fresh start. The Corgi Witness Protection Program was his ticket to a normal life, meaning a wiggle party with lots of yodeling and frapping with the ducks. Walter got his lure coursing title and free rein to come into the bathroom with me every single time I went. He's had a good year.

Our biggest feat of training was Walter sitting still on my lap. No, it isn't that easy if you spent most of your time before in a crate. He'd get on my lap but then the joy, the bliss, the total euphoria was so overwhelming that he'd almost spontaneously combust. Eyeglasses got smeared, earrings flew, and shirts got torn. His love was all elbows, toenails, and spit; his love was dangerous. Now he can lean against me and last week, he fell asleep on my lap. He's home and the barking can rest.

***

I was just pretending to be asleep. Only resting my eyes.

***

I was thinking of how we would celebrate this year of living loudly with Walter when I got the email. Warning: Rescue people never forget you. The Wyoming rescue emailed me about a Corgi in Texas. Want to know their secret weapon? They flattered me. They said he was my kind of (too much barking) dog. Like any dog still breathing isn't my kind of dog.

I know tidbits about his past: He and another stray came into a pound together. Herding dogs are famously bad in pounds, not that any breed is good. The Texas rescue stepped in to help. The Corgi got his name during the stay there. It seems the good people at the shelter thought perhaps he liked the sound of his own voice just a bit too much. She named him Preacher Man. Uh-huh.

After the usual vet visit, complete with a check-up, shots, and the hormonal nip and tuck, Preacher was ready for a new home. He was adopted with full disclosure to a someone looking for an agility prospect. And returned a few weeks later. Being a domestic animal is tough; settling in after a string of changes is even tougher.

***

Where is she? I can't breathe… Where is my human? No… Where is she?

***

See it from their side: When a herding dog gets separated from his herd, whether by accident or intention, it means he has failed the job he was born to do. That's a horrible mistake for a dog with a Type A instinct. It's enough to make you bark hysterically until you are so hysterical you can't stop barking. Then more separation, and naturally, more barking. And finally, if getting moved around starts to be a habit, a dog could lose track of his own heart. What if he is barking to be found?

Like it's the worst thing that he likes the sound of his own voice. My clients will tell you that I'm the exact same way. And that's not all we have in common; we both hate vacuum cleaners... passionately. And yes, his relationship history is a bit checkered and mine... well, you know where I'm headed with this. I've had dogs with better morals and personal habits than mine, and to tell the truth, it was like living with someone else's spinster aunt. I'll take a bad dog any day.

***

She gets me. Yay, yap, hooray, yap.

***

Preacher has some things he needs to say. I listen, not that my hearing loss doesn't come in handy sometimes. Reward the good and ignore the rest, and with some patience, his confidence will grow and so will the spaces between the barks.

We talk about this in horse rescue as well; a lot of animals are just one bad behavior away from people giving up on them. If owners would patiently try again, maybe get some advice from a trainer, things could turn around pretty quickly.

I know there are Corgis in local rescues that need homes, and I'm not sure how I got involved with this interstate Corgi trafficking thing, but I met Preacher Man at the airport. It was a silent, soulful ride home in the truck, sizing each other up. "Good boy." I said, all the way back.

Walter and Preacher Man recognized each other immediately. They sleep like brothers under my desk, they share concerns about the barn chaos when I go out to feed, and they use a team approach to keep me safe in the bathroom.

★

You check her underwear and I'll block the door.

★

I know what you're thinking: A gray-haired woman who rides horses and has a growing a pack of yodeling Corgis underfoot… That's right. I am becoming the Queen of England.

YOUR VALENTINE, EDGAR RICE BURRO

This year our Valentine message is from Edgar Rice Burro. No, don't be silly. Of course, he doesn't take over my studio and type his profound and uplifting messages with his own hooves. That would be impossible for him to do and you'd be crazy to believe it. Besides, he's much smarter than that. Edgar Rice Burro uses mind control to make me type it out. May we continue?

***

I have a deep affection for the human species. Some animals think humans have no intellect; that they have no soul, but I disagree. I think humans are trainable. I also think they are cute with hats on.

***

Valentine's Day is an odd holiday to equines who are not all that into chocolate.

***

A holiday about love is okay. There are lots of things I love: a good dirt bath after a grooming, fresh baby grass in the spring, a long and sensual ear massage during muck time... but I want to remind you humans that equines value respect over love when it comes to partners.

Human love is fickle: Right at the beginning, love requires a fall. You know, fall in love? How do you trust something that starts out of balance? And then, love matches can break up, people can take up new love interests, children can think they out-grow your love. You could be taken for granted. Once that happens, assumptions begin to take the place of honest conversation. Worst of all, you could even be abandoned. Nope. Love is not prudent. Not for an equine.

***

The dictionary definition of love is an intense feeling of deep affection.

***

On the other hand, respect is meaningful; it's the language of the herd. Respect is based on actual qualities that exist in that other person or equine, like strength or confidence or intelligence. Respect is the link between partners that elevates "Gimme a carrot" to a higher level of communication like "Hello, Anna, how may we work as partners to achieve our mutual goal?" It's a relationship that gets stronger in the face of challenges of the real world. Respect is the very foundation of civilization to an equine because it defines the hierarchy of the herd and that equals everyone's safety and security. Respect finds roots in something more substantial than a particularly lovable set of long ears. (Although I certainly do have those as well.)

***

The dictionary definition of respect is to admire someone or something deeply, because of their abilities, qualities, or achievements; a feeling or understanding that someone or something is important, serious, etc., and should be treated in an appropriate way.

Donkeys are the moral compass of any barn. If you don't think so, lend Edgar your insignificantly small (no offense) ears, and reconsider.

***

I believe a strong sense of right and wrong is crucial in a relationship. I would even argue that knowing right from wrong is more important than the actions that follow. For instance, I know it's against the rules to open the gate and break out all the horses. It's a conscious decision, done with my full awareness. You never get a whiny excuse like "I didn't know we were rationing alfalfa…" or "It isn't my fault. The Grandfather Horse made me do it…" I have a moral compass, so with blunt honesty, I admit, "Of course I did it; I'm the only one smart enough to know how the clip works and the only one with a prehensile lip that can manage to do it."

***

See? He's right. You don't have to agree with him, but you have to kind of respect him.

***

Humans are such dreamers, and although equines have always loved their human's dreams, that only goes so far. Living the dream means mutual respect. You have to show me the respect of acknowledging me and my quirks if the dream is to become real. Your dream is not all about you. The first step is to remember that every living entity deserves respect. Especially donkeys.

So, if you are wondering what your equine would like this Valentine's Day, I suggest some honest respect. Take time to acknowledge the traits you most admire and reflect in each other: Confident generosity, a sense of humor, and a commitment to positive partnership. Honor your shared strength and amazing capabilities and respect your personalities and limitations, as well.

After the important stuff, if there is some affection that needs expressing, just for the record, I like apples best.

***

Edgar Rice Burro... what he said.

BEING POST-MATURE IN THE SPRING

It's a Grandfather spring. Those words don't go together well, any more than watching elderly horses in the freshness of the season. I wouldn't trade a moment. My Grandfather Horse survived the winter to see another birthday. After our emergency vet call in November, I worried. I'm happy to report no more high drama about ... well, it's a bit embarrassing... his "emergency" sheath cleaning.

And it's finally spring. You can tell because the wind is catapulting tumbleweeds instead of snow most of the time.

My Grandfather Horse and I have a game we play every spring. Just when the grass is its best—that time just after a spring blizzard and just before the hot midday sun scorches baby grasses crisp—I accidentally-on-purpose forget to close his gate. Silly me. And he moves like a serpent, slowly to the gate, then flings it hard with his nose and squeals as he gallops out, tail flagged and proud, with his tiny herd of mares in hot pursuit. He is always incredulous at my foolishness and his good luck.

My Grandfather Horse got retired for cause, a tendon injury that took months of stall rest to heal, giving his arthritis time to cripple him. Watching him canter on two lame legs and a very weak back was frightening to watch, and there was always hang-over soreness the next day. But it was so worth it for that annual desperado's escape.

He gave up his wobbly canter a few years ago for a

bone-jarring trot. I don't let the mares join in anymore; it would hurry him too much. And last year, he made his annual escape at a walk. I'll be kind and call it a race walk, but his hooves barely cleared the ground and his legendary tail was quiet.

This year the birthday break-out day came, and I didn't latch the gate as I left to muck another run. My Grandfather Horse stood still, eyes half closed in the morning sun. I pushed the gate wider and still he took no notice. Finally, I walked up to him and scratched a handful of long, gray hairs loose. I turned but he didn't follow, so I slipped a twine around his neck and waited for him to shift his weight into a walk. We sauntered out together.

Our pasture is prairie grass, some sage, a few cacti. There is only one really exceptional patch of grass on the place. You know the kind; wider leaves and so moist it smells sweet. We made our way to the place behind the horse trailer with the special grass and I let loose of the twine. He walked a few steps and dropped his head, not even a rush now.

It was a slow morning so I plopped down to the ground to keep him grazing company. I did what I always do; I reminisced with him. Remember how afraid you were when we met? Remember sharing watermelon at horse shows? Remember that way you had of kicking me in the arch of my foot when I over-cued flying changes?

The Grandfather Horse retired ten years ago but the first couple of years where the worst. He was angry that I quit him. It was me; quitting was something he would never consider. The injury didn't matter; he was right and I could barely meet his eye. He refused to stand for the curry. We were both depressed.

Spring is the time of year for grand plans. Reclining there on the grass, I thought about what I'd like to accomplish with my young mare this year, ideas I have for my clients and the horses here for training. I notice I don't have any plans with this grand old man. *I do nothing with him.*

We aren't a young herd anymore. Some of us are literally or

figuratively old goats. My Grandfather Horse and I have much more history than future. It hurts to admit but it's agonizingly undeniable that our best days are not ahead. Some of our favorite friends, his contemporaries, are not with us this spring. We can't feel lucky when others are mourning.

But we are here now and the smell of the grass being crushed by what teeth the Grandfather Horse has left is still sweet. I fold my arms behind my head and as clouds gather, I remind my good boy of our favorite freestyle—a combination reining and dressage, to music by Bob Wills and Patsy Cline. He was nibbling grass right by my ear and his crusty old eye twinkled. Every single dream has come true. Just then the wind kicked up, with hail this time. As we ambled back to the barn, my grand plan for him came to me:

This summer I am going to *do nothing with him*—much more often.

WALTER SINGS THE SONGS OF HIS PEOPLE

My friend Sarah says, "All dog stories end the same way." I know what she means. None of us humans are getting out alive either. There is nothing remarkable about death. It's as common as dirt.

Disclaimer: No tissues allowed. Really, this time especially, if you are going to get all maudlin on me, and just stop reading now. This is not a sad story.

I haven't written about Walter for a while. He's a Corgi who came here from Wyoming to rescue us from our own self-importance eighteen months ago. His previous family found him ridiculously energetic and totally lacking an indoor voice, so naturally he settled in here fine. He's taken up duck mind-control and lure coursing.

Walter had an appointment to have his teeth cleaned last summer. During the routine blood test, his liver numbers were *four hundred times* higher than normal. I thought *my* heart would stop. But Walter, always one to look on the bright side, didn't have to get the tooth scrape after all. Not a bad day.

In the next weeks, he lost four of his meager twenty pounds. He was thin to start, so he lost muscle. His little heart-shaped backside became bony, a tail appeared, and his ears became wider than his shoulders.

We changed his diet to a special home-cooked concoction that is both time-consuming to make and expensive. Walter gets four or five meals a day, over six cups total. He's on a variety of scary medications, each of them timed awkwardly from the others. Now feeding involves math skills but most of his weight has returned. Of course, Walter would like you to imagine the joy—the absolute bliss—of following his human into the kitchen and getting fed *every single time*. Not all the dogs, just him! How great is that?!

The vet told me there were two liver maladies possible, one that's manageable with medication and one that's terminal. Biopsy results were slow returning from the lab because Walter manages to have both conditions. A year later, he doesn't let it get in the way of his master plan for a bunny-free farm.

When Walter was celebrating his one-year Gotcha Day, we received a call from the Corgi Witness Protection Program about a Texas Corgi who *over-spoke* to his rescuers and needed a *verbally tolerant* home. Preacher Man joined us. I worried at first that it would be hard on Walter in his diminished state; maybe they wouldn't get along. Silly me. They immediately recognized each other as twin brothers from different puppy mills and the party started.

The non-stop chatter is back; the sing-song hum, the Corgi-quack, the how-oo-ling. I feel Walter following me so close that his chest bumps my heel with each stride. They both saw a pattern and wisely decided to call truce and unilateral retreat in the Cat Wars. When I notice my blue rug turn Corgi red, I know every hair trapped there is one less hair on my clothes. And sometimes when the thrill of the fourth or fifth meal is too much to bear, Walter nips my backside. It's understandable; I think his butt is pretty cute too.

The Dude Rancher and I would like to say that there is less barking. It wouldn't be true. The dogs egg each other on a bit but we're teaching them to whisper. I would like to say that it's a huge success. It's more like a work in progress but the Dude Rancher and I are whispering more.

And if the coyotes are at the pond, Walter and Preacher

Man join in, with snouts high and ears dropped back over their shoulders. They close their eyes and yodel the prairie opera with reckless soprano abandon. What's a little barking but praise of life?

When Walter first came here, he was human-starved. Holding him on my lap was like holding a spit-filled hurricane. He was too excited to do anything but lick and spin. Preacher didn't spin on my lap. He was more like an out-of-water Walleye but with the same passion for lap dancing.

But now being close is more of a slow dance. Sometimes we have a nap for lunch. There's an initial scurry to see who can get the coveted place closest to my head, but Walter and Preacher Man both stretch out on my torso and we dog-pile. We steal a half an hour and as I come awake, sometimes we're all breathing together. One of us might snore. Other times I can feel a heartbeat in my chest so close that I don't know whose it is.

Here is my one dog training tip: When they ask for my attention, I give it to them.

Some of my friends who know Walter's diagnosis think he was lucky to find us. Hogwash. I think it's the other way around. We're the lucky ones, schooled by someone as filled with live-fast, love-hard joy as Walter. We aren't getting any younger either.

Walter has us all right where he wants us. Sometimes he leaps on a visitor's lap with a wide-eared innocent look and a big smile, and asks, "Have you heard I'm dying?" It's crazy but people think that makes him special and he works it for all he's worth. Smart boy.

Please don't feel sorry for Walter. We are riding the fast train; we are living for the moment. One day he will be gone and it won't be news. But we do have big news today. Walter is barking to high heaven and zealously alive.

Dying is sad and ordinary. Walter thinks living is the art that matters most. Bark more, whine less.

A MUCK MEDITATION ON BARN SWALLOWS

I feel sorry for people who don't muck. How do they find that deep satisfied breath? How do they organize their thoughts? Or find peace of heart with the city-world?

This time of the year the birds are especially distracting. There's some serious competition in the sky; I have to love the hawks as they hang motionless in the air, watching my farm and giving a plaintive call to the prairie. The pond is totally alive with chatter. There's always a *quackle* of ducks with tails up in the air. Herons stalk the edge, stiff with caution. They keep a wary distance and are timeless when airborne, coasting on the wind like pterodactyls.

Each spring Canada geese march around my pond, stretching their necks tall, checking the neighborhood to see if it's a worthy nest area. We had never passed the test before but this year a mated pair hatched four eggs. The goslings all survived and are teen-aged now. Their markings make them look over-dressed but then Canada geese have always been more formal.

Swallows might be my favorite barn bird. They have one wing in both worlds: They're wild birds who choose to live with domestic animals. Like mice and rabbits, they appreciate sharing the barn with horses and goats. But it isn't just affection; it's an exchange of goods and services. They barter for rent of a rafter, paid for with active insect control.

Barn swallows are a little fancier than they need to be. Their body angles look like live Sumi brush paintings. They disdain everyday brown feathers for a sophisticated color choice: shiny midnight blue back and wings, and a dapper apricot-colored vest. Long fringe tail feathers on the males seem impractical for daily barn chores, but they are fanatic workers and committed parents.

I get a lot of close-up time with the barn swallows while mucking. The first nest was in the big barn over the hay with a clear shot at the door, safe and practical. Then the next year they built a nest in the smaller barn but they didn't even put eggs in that one. Finally, two years ago they worked to build a perfect nest of mud and horse tail hair, cemented to an eave above the Grandfather Horse's run. They rest on the fence panels and seem to prefer his company. Who can blame them?

Once the hatchlings are all un-shelled, their bright yellow rubbery-rimmed beaks are wider than their heads. They're screaming-ready to eat and the parents frantically rush to feed them. Swallows are insectivores who fly as much as six hundred miles a day feeding their young. Soon the parents both looked worse for the wear; skinny and a bit flapped out.

The babies peer over the side of the nest with their noggins all in a row. As the fledglings near leaving the nest, the parents' swooping attacks become more frequent and furious toward anyone coming near the barn. It might work against them: As the parents are frantically trying to clear the way to keep the babies safe, it's that same frantic activity that alerts us that the babies will be out soon.

The swallow parents are hyper-protective, staring me down as I muck under their nest. The diligent parenting works and a high percentage of their babies survive. I envy these birds their instinct; not all humans share it. Flying like tiny fighter jets, they go back to making strafing runs over my barn cats.

Since mouse season is already in full swing, the cats have been coming and going from the barn like factory workers with their wiggling time cards clenched in their teeth, on the way to the picnic table under the tree which everyone agrees is the best place for tormenting mice. The cats pretend to ignore the birds who have no more meat on them than a moth. Swallows are not fooled for a moment.

Soon the day comes that the babies glide out of the nest and follow the parents to the metal panels that make my round pen. It's a perfect flight training field. The adults stand guard while the young fliers flap and glide from one side to the other, getting steadier each hour. The family is all there until the exhausted fledglings return to the nest.

In a day or two the strafing runs stop and I know the babies are steady on the wing. Now the nest is empty but the sky is full. The young ones look like their feathers are too big for them but at least they are finally growing into their beaks. Edgar Rice Burro and I take a break from mucking to watch them soaring over the pond, sweeping up insects. Do birds feel joy? How can they not?

They are all air and feathers; gravity has no pull. They soar above and glide below the other birds, and we all watch. Ducks have thick wet webbed feet and the heron's bony knees stick out, no matter how tightly they fold them. The Grandfather Horse sleeps in the sun and I linger over my muck. Only swallows fly like jet-propelled kites, with a high-speed flip-change of direction on a whim, coasting the pond surface for juicy bugs. They even eat with just a bit more flair than need be.

Compared to grander birds, swallows are probably no big deal. But I marvel, I envy, I lose time watching the miracle again each year. Why colors so bright in the barn's dust and dirt? Why so much art on the wing? Such a small life yet protected so ferociously.

Free as a bird, goes the old saying. The horses and I never take it for granted. *Liberty.*

DONKEYS FOR PEACE: EDGAR RICE BURRO

It was the geldings day for the south pasture, the best turnout spot. They are athletic boys who like to start with a few wind sprints. Then somebody pretends to be afraid of something invisible and they bolt off sideways, bucking and farting and air kicking. It's all good clean fun.

Edgar Rice Burro was waiting at the gate to join them with Bhim, a thirty-four-inch-tall miniature horse here for training from a local rescue. Edgar helps me with the rescue horses who visit. He's good at sharing and has a soft heart for strangers. He is slow to react to insults and conservative about name calling. Always ready to forgive and looking for a friend, Edgar doesn't hold with bigotry. He's kind to mares and geldings alike, with no breed preference. Being Edgar isn't a bad thing.

Edgar knew Bhim was special from the beginning but it took a long time to make friends. The little horse had a chip on his shoulder and liked to throw his insignificant weight around. Bhim wasn't good at socializing. He wanted to join in but his fear got in the way. Edgar and I chipped away and eventually we wore Bhim down. We were relentless.

I finally opened the gate after the geldings were done playing, and Edgar and Bhim trotted out and immediately threw their heads down and started grazing. Neither of them had any plans to lift their heads for the next four hours. It was no big deal; they'd all been turned out together in the same pen before. Sure, this was the wide-open pasture but we're all friends here.

I looked out a second later and everyone was running. I smiled at the sight: Beautiful horses, different strides, and little Bhim proudly out front. Everyone seemed good, but no. Something changed. Someone pushed ahead, someone else pinned his ears. I'm not sure who started it but suddenly the herd turned mean. Bhim was running tense and panicked. The big geldings were racing after him, necks long and teeth bared. It didn't stop; they were running Bhim off his feet. I grabbed a rope to swing, like that would make a difference in this free-for-all.

By the time I got through the gate, Edgar had joined in. He was running hard, right behind Bhim. Shame on him. I expected so much better from an animal of his intellect and compassion.

The galloping herd fought for position; Bhim was barely in front. His tail was tucked tight. Would they run him over? Grab him by the neck and shake him? Could Bhim survive a stampede?

Then I saw Edgar. He had his nose to the inside and was gently suggesting that Bhim move to the outside. Bhim didn't take the cue right off—he was breathing hard and in a panic. *Run. Just run.* In the meantime, Edgar's hind swung from side to side. The three huge geldings were bumping into him but he didn't give way. Edgar was blocking like a linebacker. No one was getting past him.

Finally, Bhim could slow, first down to a trot and then a walk, while Edgar kept the big boys behind him. Bhim looked exhausted; he blew and shook his head. Easy to act like a big stud now. He fooled no one but Edgar didn't mind. This little horse had every right to celebrate. Edgar doesn't hold with *belittling* others just to make yourself bigger.

Don't feel too bad for Bhim. Not a mark on him and now he and Edgar get turnout with the mares. Bhim has always fancied himself to have a way with the mares (whereas Edgar actually does).

These are challenging days. World politics are pretty adversarial. It's been a hard summer on my extended herd, too. Some of us are facing physical challenges. Some of us are being bullied. Some of us are just worn out by bad luck and feeling chased by circumstances beyond our control. It's a good time to have a saintly burro on your side. Or maybe get your ass in the way and slow things down to a more civilized pace.

Donkeys are misunderstood. When people behave badly, we call them asses. The truth is, more of us should defend our friends, stop bullying, and set a good example by holding to kindness when the crowd goes stupid. More of us should stubbornly hold on to our best self. Like a real ass.

A COWGIRL LOOKS (SQUINTS) AT SIXTY

I notice I wear my glasses in the shower more often these days. Unintentionally. I mention it because as I write this, it's my sixtieth birthday and I had a revelation in the shower. Wait, it gets worse.

I've decided it's time to start riding naked. Who's in? Naked Dressage. It's an idea whose time has come. Anybody? Okay, I understand that dressage has a stuffy reputation and I'm forever defending it—but think about it. It might be just what the sport needs. Really, no one wants to ride with me? How about spectators? No? None?

I'm shocked. (Not.) If the truth be told, no women look good riding naked at any age. (Fashion shots don't count; I'm talking *actual* riding.) A person of my calendar accumulation and... dimensional quality, least of all. And I couldn't be more pleased. One of the very best things about being sixty is that no one *wants* to see me naked—on a horse or anywhere else. That makes me really happy. Liberated. Free. The meat wagon has left. Friends I have now love me without cosmetic correction, for the same reason horses and dogs have from the beginning. It's dependable.

But back to the shower. Is revelation a bad word choice? I was surveying the *landscape* and thinking about skin. I remember waking up on my fiftieth birthday and noticing that someone had switched the skin on my forearms. I was more confused than outraged, but it was undeniable. My midlife skin was gone and left in its place was some *old lady* skin that was looking desert-dry and a bit hacked up. My arm hairs practically had split ends. It was a crime.

In the last decade, there's been more lawlessness. My neck has developed a wattle, when I squint in the sun my eyes totally disappear inside my *happy* wrinkles, and the tops of my hands have turned into torn and bruised parchment. I won't mention, in this marginally polite company, what's happened under my shirt, but they make B-grade disaster movies about less.

We women keep plastic surgeons rich, while we go nuts about our skin aging. It's easy to feel squeezed by the grip of judgment from a critical culture, who would like women to stay contained in tight skins. And it's an equal opportunity betrayal of women of all sizes, careers, income, and of course, numbers of cats. Even rebels who left the cosmetic circus years ago are forced to notice when squinting creates temporary blindness.

I have a ridiculously optimistic question I ask myself when everything looks like a huge disaster: *What if this isn't wrong?* And the answer about my skin came to me in the shower.

When I was younger, my skin had to hold it all together. My brains scattered all the time and my heart was always breaking. Sometimes I puked my guts out. My feet marched off in bad directions and my hands should have stayed in my pockets more than they did. My skin had the nearly impossible job of holding me together.

These days my skin slouches around me. I look like a pasty, white basset hound, with rolls of this and that migrating to the oddest places. At first I thought my skin had lost its grip, but that's not it. I think now, at sixty, my skin trusts me more. That's what all the sagging and bagging and general lumpiness is about: Trust and maybe it's gained some confidence in me as well.

My brain stays steady now for the most part. It used to

explode about a dozen times a day but I've gained some tolerance for change. My body stays in line, a little stiff some days, but like they say, if something didn't hurt when I got up in the morning, I'd think I was dead.

My heart used to need both skin and ribs to protect it. At this point, I've had a huge herd of horses stomping around in there for so long that it's all stretched out and softened. It's been padded with dog hair and sure, there's a hole left when I lose a friend, but the truth is my heart has been so enlarged by loving all of them in the first place, that I survive. Like stretched out socks, there is always room for more; I like my heart better this way.

Feeling comfortable in your own skin can't be over-rated. It's good horsemanship; probably the thing horses and dogs notice about us first. It's not a crime to pack a few years on. We should wear it with the confidence of an old sweatshirt and be proud: sagging isn't a failure of our skin, but really it's the opposite. It's a compliment when your skin says, "Good job, you can hold your own self together now."

I also notice from time to time that I've sprouted a thick hair or two on my chin, just above my wattle. They are white and coarse… it's good news; I'm sure this means I'm turning into a horse. Evolution is a wonder.

I'm not special, just one more in a herd of feisty old cowgirls who are not anywhere near done yet. I just want to say thank you on this birthday, to all the horses and dogs who gave my skin a reason to relax. They've taught me well, especially my Grandfather Horse. It isn't just great to be alive. It's great to be so…so…*ripe*.

A CALL TO ARMS—OR HOOVES

You've had this happen. Someone finds out you have a horse and they ask, "Do you know my sister's friend, Diane? She has a horse." Like there are eleven of us in the state.

People who own horses are a wide and diverse group. We divide ourselves by breed and riding discipline. Some of us crave the camaraderie of competition and some of us "only trail ride." And we have strong opinions about it, not that it matters.

Some of us are big talkers and small doers. Some of us just work with rescues. We started with horses when we were so young that we can't remember a time we weren't horse-crazy. Some of us set ourselves free at forty-five or fifty with a midlife first horse.

Some of us have good hands and some of us just think we do. Some of us know everything and some of us hope to be taking lessons forever. Some of us fight with horses because we think it's the only way. Some of us give up riding because our horses are so unresponsive to us.

I know it's crazy but in the world of people who own horses, not everyone cares about horses all that much. You can tell by their words and actions. There are numbers of professional trainers who don't even particularly like horses, much less respect them.

And some of us don't tell the truth as a matter of habit.

Do you know the difference between people who own horses and a real horse-person? The thing to notice immediately about the horse-person moniker is the word *horse* comes first, and not by random coincidence.

Horse-*people* are a sub-species of horses, not humans. At some point, they changed teams and being human became less important. It's a disease, a mental affliction that infects the entire body, from our fixated brains to our manure-coated boots. The pre-teen years are the worst: We can't sleep and spend a lot of time pretend-cantering around the house.

A few horse-crazy girls grow into horse-people, which is even more insufferable. Like micro-managing drug addicts, we obsess about hoof angle or saddle fit. We go on about bits and supplements and what our horses do in turnout. The Dude Rancher, who tires of horse conversation after ten minutes or so, will tell you we are only fit company for other horse-people. He's right.

Some of our rides are euphoric, but many are just fundamental communication. Trying to understand and asking the same in return. We have big dreams and low expectations, happy for every good stride. Nothing is more important than the health and soundness of our equine partner.

We treat our elders with respect. The old campaigners who taught us how to ride, the kind boss mare who gave birth to champions, the sweet gelding who takes care of kids: It isn't that we treat them like family members. They *are* family members.

We adjust our lives to suit our horses and make each of our life decisions with them a priority. People who are blessed with horses *and* money make it look easy. It's a bit trickier without a trust fund, but we find a way. We change careers, we give up vacations. We do without less important things and don't whine about it. After all, they are *less important* things.

Because we are just like our horses, we tend to be a physically tough bunch, not afraid of work or dirt or poop. But on the inside, we belong to the herd. We're mush, sweetness, and a weathered hand on a patch of hair. We protect our horse-crazy hearts by being tough, and the mushier we are on the inside, the more defensive of the horse on the outside.

We always save our best for horses.

At the end of the day, hands crack, feet ache, and there is that honest exhaustion that comes from work well done. We slump on the sofa with a couple of dogs and cats and that old movie comes on the TV. We've seen it a hundred times. It's one from the genre labeled Horse-Crazy Girl Movies, like *Black Beauty* or *The Man from Snowy River* or *Seabiscuit*. We hunker down and when the scenes come where the horses gallop in slow motion, for the hundredth time, we tear up. We will never stop any of it. Horses are in our blood.

How to get on the bad side of a horse-woman? Easy question, be cruel to any animal, but especially a horse. Acting from a place of personal convenience over animal welfare will not be tolerated, any more than parents who put their own desires above their children's needs.

But even horse-people know we can't save them all. Of course, we still try. We must try.

A week ago, a good dog led the way to the discovery of fourteen horses dead on the ground and another ten surviving among the remains in a barn a few miles away in Black Forest. The woman who followed her dog into the barn called the sheriff and the press. Smart.

I am not going to rehash the gory details one more time. You don't have to be a horse-person to recognize this level of brutal neglect. There was so much wrong, fundamentally wrong, before lye was dumped on the carcasses and then covered by tarps. It started so much smaller than that.

And sadly, too many horse-people have struggled with the sheriff's office in an effort to get our weak animal-welfare laws enforced. Horse rescues don't fare much better than individuals.

Here is the good news: This is one time when complaining helped. Horse-people stood up for what was left of this herd, all over the world. We loudly signed petitions; thousands of us called and emailed county officials. I am so proud. Press releases from the sheriff's department *defensively* defend their actions but at the same time it's obvious that given the chance, this incident would have been swept under the rug like so many others.

We didn't let them. We came out of our home barns and spoke up in such huge numbers that things changed. The surviving horses got help. It was a small victory in the big picture but with our foot in the door, it is also no time to back off. Horse-people need to push ahead with stronger animal-welfare laws and enforcement. We can do more.

My point is not to rant about who loves horses the most. What I'm hoping is that in the shadow of this horrific incident more people who own horses will cross the line and become horse-people. In your heart, you know where you stand. Are you holding back? Is there more you can give?

If you are a horse-person, now is the time to put the muck fork down and speak up.

Maybe the biggest fact a horse-person accepts is that no matter how great the commitment we have, no matter how much time and money and sweat we happily offer our own horses and horses out in the world, we will always be asked to give more. And then, one more time, we will have to dig deep from the infinite well of passion and purpose horses have given us, and find a way to do even more—graciously and generously. We learned that from horses, too.

PIONEER SPIRIT:
A MESSAGE FROM LEAFA

Leafa Numbers was my paternal grandmother. She was born in 1888 in a sod shanty in Kansas.

We had a belated chat this week. A graduate student doing research about the pioneers who settled North Dakota interviewed some nursing home residents in 1976. I got a tape of my grandmother's interview back then and my cassette player promptly ate it. Technology returned her to me this week, in the form of a CD. I would have recognized her voice anywhere.

My great-grandfather Elias Numbers was just a bit too young to fight in the Civil War, like his older brother did. After he married and started a family, they moved from Kansas to Iowa in a covered wagon, then on to Illinois where he lost his wife and two of his daughters to typhoid fever. Then on to Missouri. Leafa hired out to work for other families and never finished school.

The interviewer asked if she knew how poor they were. She answered, "We knew work and hard times. He [her father] had nothing to give but he was good to us."

Then at seventeen, she and her sister caught a ride in a covered wagon headed to North Dakota. They heard land was cheap and they could make their fortunes there. They both hired out to work on a cook cart. "I was always a big girl and I wore a long skirt so I could earn women's wages." That was four dollars a day for the two of them and when she said *big girl*, her voice lifted. She was bragging.

She met a Canadian, Percy Blake. He was a farmer and a horseman and eighteen years old. He had a Flying Dutchman Plow and a team of good horses. They married the next year, 1906.

Leafa and Percy moved a few times but finally settled on a farm and raised a big garden, chickens, pigs, cattle, and five kids. Percy contracted to build local roads, driving a five-abreast team with a grating plow to earn extra money. "He was a hustler and I was a good manager. I delivered more colts and calves than any woman in North Dakota," she said.

"The thirties pert'near broke us." A reminder; this was a few miles from Canada. The winters were brutal even before the Great Depression knocked everyone down. She took pride, "But I always set a good table." Farm talk for no one went hungry.

"We had good horses." She said it a few times during the interview. It was what put them ahead. A couple of times a year, they sold a horse for a hundred dollars. "That was a lot of money in those days," she said. And Percy sold one horse for three thousand dollars but before she could explain, the interviewer changed topics, leaving me wildly curious. Percy had a reputation as a horse trader, but who did he sell to for that much? What horse?

The interviewer asked if it was hard being a pioneer mother. "Well, there was a saying; North Dakota was hell on women and horses." She had a self-deprecating laugh and as easy as common sense, she said, *"It was a tough life if you was useless."* This might be my new mantra.

Percy had passed several years earlier and when the interviewer asked Leafa about re-marrying, "Oh, I should say not... My gosh, you get tired of waitin' on men."

"I'm satisfied." She said that more than a few times during the interview, too. She was satisfied with her life, boasted that none of her family ever got in trouble with the law, and was proud that she and her husband had built something. She had mastered the art of wanting what she had.

When Leafa called Percy a good hustler, I'm not sure of her meaning but my grandfather became a local horse-trading legend, wealthy by farm standards. He retired to smoke stinky cigars and shoot ducks out the window of his big black Cadillac. Satisfied.

I didn't see my grandparents often but our family visited just before Grandpa Blake died. They were living in town then, in the nicest house I'd ever been in. Grandma kept store-bought canned apricot juice in the fridge and she poured some into a small painted glass for me. It was sweet and thick; I held it in my mouth to make it last longer.

Why does any of this matter?

Hearing Leafa's voice, *at this age*, it's easy to see how much alike we are. I'm grateful to live by and for good horses, too. It's good to be reminded that I'm just a step or two from being a pioneer of this young country. I come from strong stock, not afraid of hard work. If you read too many dressage magazines, it can seem like the best horse traditions are European but America has a dynamic history with horses from the beginning. Don't sell us—or our horses—short.

The last time I saw my grandmother was just after this interview. I was twenty-two and she was eighty-nine. I meant to flatter her by asking about the interview and the covered wagon trip from Missouri north. For a moment, she got distracted by a memory too juicy to share with the interviewer. She smiled like a girlfriend and her pale blue eyes lit up. She said she worked at a boarding house, and the James boys used to drop by to get their dinner and flirt with the womenfolk in the kitchen. My head spun. That was the way our family referred to people; the Blake boys... the Johnson boys...

"Grandma, Frank and Jesse?" I asked, in the most incredulous voice ever.

"Yes, dearie, but that's a different story. Now, that wagon trip…"

GOLDEN DAYS AND HINDSIGHT GUILT

These late October days are golden—sweet and rich, and as temporary as a long, crisp leaf. The sun is slow to rise and takes its time setting over Pikes Peak. The clouds hold onto its colorful tail, long after the sun is gone. The horses and I want to languish on the tight wire between Indian summer and what comes next for as long as we can. We know this is the lull before the storm.

My Grandfather Horse got through last winter stronger than I thought he would, but it wasn't pretty. The cold makes him stiff and he doesn't want to move. If he doesn't move, his arthritis gets worse and hurts more, so then he moves less. It's a vicious circle.

He doesn't complain, he's a stoic guy, but I never get over the feeling of a vice-grip crushing my chest. Relief came with spring, but as soon as he started shedding his winter coat, his weight dropped as well. I didn't worry at first, since he was eating well. The weight loss was gradual, until it wasn't.

One day he was nearly skeletal. Like a neglected, abandoned horse. How did this happen *on my watch!* I confess—it hurt me to just look at him. I had a huge fit of Hindsight Guilt. Have you had it?

Hindsight Guilt is when you think you're doing your best but you get a diagnosis, or learn something new, or come up with a better technique, for the care or riding or understanding of your horse, and then impale yourself on a pike for the suffering you've caused by your own stupid ignorance. Even if the thing you learn is new technology, even if you are doing a better job than any human possibly could, Hindsight Guilt hits and in that moment, you call yourself the ultimate curse: *Abuser*.

Of course, I had him checked out. His list of chronic ailments is long. The diagnosis? He's old. Gradual degeneration is expected. My vet said I was doing everything right.

But still, he was eating and losing weight. His chronic diarrhea lessened to intermittent diarrhea, a huge improvement. I'm not one for any sort of fecal-phobia. I read manure like tarot cards. It's my go-to standard health predictor. I poked my way through and it seemed, somehow, that the hay was not breaking down as well as the other horse's manure. It was a tiny, almost invisible difference. Too much information? Not if it's your horse.

So, I tweaked his feed again. It's constant with an old horse. I resist the sticky senior feeds with molasses so thick that the grain freezes solid. Grain isn't that good for most horses in the first place. Having said that, I was feeding some healthy senior feed without molasses, alfalfa pellets, beet pulp, and free choice hay. Along with anything else I could think of. He continued to lose weight. I continued to tweak.

My Hindsight Guilt would like to have a word: *"She's an idiot. She thought because he was eating hay that he was getting some nutrient value. He wasn't. I repeat––she's an idiot."*

I saw weight gain finally, by feeding more soaked alfalfa-grass pellets than I thought any horse could possibly eat. It's science. Pellets have tiny particles that are easier for an old horse to utilize. He gets one flake of hay to play with but he doesn't eat it.

And now he's pudgy. I can't feel his ribs, and even old and sway-backed with more arthritis than bone, he has gotten bright-eyed. It's been years, but he's being mischievous again. He gives the farrier lip and pulls his hoof away; we both grin like school-girls. Sometimes the Grandfather Horse even trots. We all stop and applaud him.

This fall, the equine dentist told me the Grandfather Horse

had lost teeth. I reminded him my horse had one tooth pulled three years back. "Nope, more than that one," the dentist said. "Not many teeth left on that side at all." It was hindsight news to me.

Wouldn't I have seen the teeth on the ground? If they were hidden in his manure, I would've found them with my CSI manure skills. I scrutinize this horse; how did they get by me? More Hindsight Guilt but as usual, the self-name-calling doesn't help.

This is the strongest my Grandfather Horse has been in the fall for years. Don't get me wrong, he's still dead lame. But he has gotten a second wind. He has his sense of humor back. I am beyond grateful, but not at all happy because of another attack of Hindsight Guilt. It's chronic with me and this horse. I've had it since I started riding him decades ago.

For now, we have Indian summer. It isn't just the time of year—it's his time of life. These are his golden days, precious for their fragility. Precious because we do know the future.

His eye-sight has degenerated. He's frightened of his own shadow. Deeply, profoundly, with sincere honesty, he is afraid. I can respect that. It's a good opportunity to go slower and reward more. He taught me that.

The challenge with the elders is to separate the old age issues that you can't help from the ones you can. And then when you do help something, survive the Hindsight Guilt about not doing better, faster, more perfectly.

Because these Grandfather Horses deserve more than our best, every single day. They taught us, they lifted us up, and they gave us to ourselves in a way no one else could have. We owe them.

If I live another hundred years, I will always have Hindsight Guilt that I could not do for him even a fraction of what he did for me. And that's just where he wants me.

WEATHER AMNESIA:
A TIME-CHANGE RAGE

"Do not go gentle into that good night,
Old age should burn and rave at close of day;
Rage, rage against the dying of the light." —Dylan Thomas

Scholars will tell you that this Dylan Thomas poem is about old age and death. It's a little-known fact, probably made up, that this poem was actually not written by Dylan Thomas at all, but rather his riding instructor who penned it at the fall time-change.

The poem is actually about (line 1) not going home to a warm dinner after work, followed by wine and a good book, but instead, (line 2) flame on—you're no spring chicken and horse lives are short—ride anyway, and (line 3) scream and holler, then drive the truck over to the arena and angle the headlights down the long side. Turn up the radio while you're at it.

The first thing you notice living on the prairie is that there isn't a lot to distract you from the weather. Especially now; it's Indian summer and glorious. We had a hard frost and celebrated death to the flies. Dawn and dusk are quiet baby colors—pinks, blues, yellows. The leaves on our scant trees are a metallic copper, crackling in the breeze. There is a delicate quality to the outdoors just now. It's like the earth is holding its breath, waiting for the wind from the north. Any minute that wind will howl us naked and mono-chromatic till spring.

There is this golden afternoon when you look into your horse's eye and take a moment to reflect back and harvest the gains you have made over the summer. It's too easy to forget the successes because they are always immediately followed with the next challenge. It seems every year at this time, we improve our riding in direct proportion to the number of fewer minutes of daylight per day. And then, winter detention.

Buck up. Summer has made us lazy and weak. We have no tolerance after a season of long days and warm breezes. Each fall we have to re-grow our cold weather skills again. Like the woolly mammoths our horses become, we have to bulk up with the audacity to go to the barn and *ride anyway.*

In this last week since the time change (hiss...) I've had no fewer than five people tell me that they can't ride in the winter because they don't have an indoor arena. I am not sure what's more depressing—having an hour of daylight arbitrarily taken away in the evening or the attitude that your riding is doomed because of real estate.

About this time, I start to notice that I forgot my work gloves and my hands are cold. It's still in the forties, but where are my gloves? Everyone in the barn is looking shaggy and yet I haven't put on even one extra hair. I'm unprepared.

It's time to schedule the Grandfather Horse's annual "emergency" sheath cleaning. Meaning the old ones move less in the cold and things in that area can get dangerously coagulated. He wants that sheath winterized. Enough said?

Obviously, it's time to put the tank heaters in. Dawdling on this chore has no actual effect at all on forestalling blizzards. It still feels infinitely better to break a thin layer of ice instead of giving in and admitting to the psychological issue of tank heater denial. By now I remember to put gloves on, but there are so many holes in the fingers, that it does no good anyway. Add gloves to the denial list.

The bedtime barn walk-through also includes wearing a

head lamp over my Elmer Fudd hat, but over the complaints of my toes, I will not give in to winter muck boots just yet. It's my own small "*rage against the dying of the light.*"

Attention! This is your annual reminder that the worst part of the cold is that our minds are stuck back in September. Get over it. There are people who change priorities with the seasons—but we don't put horses away for the season like a set of golf clubs. I'm right about that, aren't I?

If we took the time we spend complaining about not having an indoor arena, and used it even just doing ground-play in the pasture, we would have a better relationship with our horse by the time the days start to get longer. Consider buying some new socks. There's a direct connection between sock age and quality of life. I also recommend an extremely ugly hat with ear flaps like mine. I am not sure if they are warmer but just being seen in one makes you a stronger person. Before you know it, days will be getting longer and you will be standing around the tack room with your ice-riders talking trash about crashing the Iditarod.

It's the same every year at this time. We get a form of temporary amnesia brought on from the first north wind that hits us squarely in the face. There are a million reasons to tuck in for the winter, bake cookies, and not go to the barn. Most of them even have a ring of common sense about them. *Beware: when common sense begins to appeal to horse people, it's the beginning of the end.*

On the other side of the equation there is just one reason that you might want to buck up and go to the barn: The short life of your good horse balanced against the unknown date of your last ride together. Rage against that.

WAITING OUT THE STORM WITH THE DOGS OF WAR

Last Monday I worked a couple of horses in the morning. Then the temperature dropped in the afternoon—*by fifty-four degrees*. I raced to the feed store to get an emergency stash of senior feed and when I came out, there was a wall of black cloud from one horizon to the other, bearing down on me like a bad B-movie about zombie-locusts. Frozen zombie-locusts.

It's my fault. Last week I made fun of a Dylan Thomas poem and then chided us all for the annual loss of winter tolerance. Perish the thought. It hasn't been above ten degrees since. I got some of my chops back—it soared up to twelve degrees and I almost took one of my hats off.

So, I have been in the house all week, except to feed and have brief outdoor frozen water-hose wrestling matches. The dogs and I have cabin fever in early November. A poor sign. Also, an opportunity to update you on the Cat Sirens, aka the rescue Corgi delinquents, Walter and Preacher Man, both enthusiastic about their new careers here: It's not a job, it's an adventure.

Strange I have managed to live all these years without even one cat siren, before the Little Corgi Men came. For just the last forty-five years or so, my cats and dogs have always been friends. Until now.

Hank is no help. He is a huge cat; sack of potatoes huge. And he has a reputation.

Years ago, a friend was over with her Australian shepherd. We were all at the table, when her sweet little Aussie came barreling into the room with a loud whiny-howl and crash-landed under her owner's chair, quivering. We all looked expectantly at the doorway she just careened through, to see Hank saunter to the threshold, sit, and casually lick a paw. Music from a Clint Eastwood spaghetti western swelled in the background. (Okay, I made that last part up.)

Like a school-yard bully, Hank developed an affection for tormenting dogs. It didn't matter; none of my own dogs took him seriously.

That's until the Little Men came, dead certain that the big black dogs were stupid enough sleep though Armageddon, and that the rest of us lacked the intellect to understand the true security threat Hank and Squirrel posed.

This cat/dog war was complicated by Hank's sister, Squirrel, who is a chronic nose-butt fanatic. She can get right up to you and nearly snap off the end of your nose if you don't see her coming.

The ginger cat, Lulu, is bored by dogs and stayed in her master bedroom most days. She appeared so rarely that the Little Men think she was the ghost of a warrior princess cat, probably of Viking descent. It's complicated territory.

The war began when Walter arrived here two years ago. He immediately recognized what the rest of us had failed to see. Have I mentioned that even on this scale, war is hell? I negotiated with Walter (there is no negotiating with cats, of course) and gained a frail truce. It de-escalated to a cold war of stares and gamesmanship. It was nearly bearable.

But a year ago, reinforcements arrived. Fresh from a secret anti-cat training center/dog-pound in rural Texas, Preacher Man arrived, girded for battle. Well, actually there seems to be some question about his urinary habits, so he wears a belly band (complete with a long-lost feminine hygiene product) while inside the house. But it has a very intimidating pirate pattern to the fabric and he looks just like Stallone in it. Without the cartridge belts and a little wider in the waist. Still, very, very scary.

Walter has a grumbly old-sounding bass voice, like some-body's weird uncle who is always muttering about something just under his breath, until it percolates up to a full rib-spreading bark—an operatic bark. Preacher Man has a high, staccato Irish tenor of a bark. Like glass shattering. Like an ambulance howl.

Hank torments the Little Men with cruelty and sinister intent. He does this by sitting in the middle of the threshold, and looking away. Such insult cannot go unanswered. Hank has a wicked sit. He is tall. He never blinks. Again and again, the insult cannot go unanswered.

Hank feels invincible. He is almost thirteen years old now and only has two teeth left. He hasn't gotten this much bang for the buck in years.

And still, the door to my studio must be protected at all costs. The Little Men must hold, they must soldier on. I hear a shrill yip with each hit of toenails on linoleum, as Preacher bounds not-quite-forward toward Hank, now a safe distance away, sleeping in a basket of gloves, on top of some shelves. I make the shushing sound, and Preacher runs to me full-tilt, wiggling to see me alive and rewarding his Little Man bravery. With no time to rest, he attacks again.

Walter and Preacher Man can feel your dismissive laugh, dear reader. This is how countries become enslaved, you know. See it through their eyes. Hank is huge. They are fighting for a lifestyle here and your apathy will be your demise.

Consider yourself warmed. I mean warned.

SEASONAL TRAINING AIDS

I'll speak for myself. It's only the middle of December and I'm a bit tired of this holiday season already. It probably has something to do with the days being so short. The noon sun is so low in the southern sky that a habitual twilight-squint has settled in between my eye-brows by mid-day. It's hard to find rhythm in all the hurry and fuss. Taking a nap on your nose like the Grandfather Horse might pass as an elite act of rebellion!

As Christmas music blasts in every public place, it would be generous for the majority group to remember that not everyone celebrates this holiday. Not everyone is Christian. Not everyone has family. Not everyone can keep up. If the holiday was a trail ride, it would be good manners to slow up so it was comfortable for those with less wherewithal, rather than galloping off and abandoning them in your wake.

Even if you love the holiday, it can be an exhausting, stressful time of the year out in the real world. Not that all the stress is necessarily bad. Some of the stress is fun; annual parties, people speaking the universal language of cookies, Christmas lights strung everywhere, and family dinners. Some of the stress is not so fun; budget breaking expenses, time pressures so huge that you can already be late before dawn, the need to be endlessly cheerful, and…family dinners.

Humans like routines as much as horses, but during this month our usual routines are especially uprooted. We're torn between barn time and holiday obligations. The pressure of the outside world puts a speed requirement on every moment and life can feel like a total runaway, only the wrong direction—away from the barn.

At the same time, it's our daily routines and rituals that truly keep us polite and reasonably sane. As we have less time and more demands—our healthy routines are usually the first to go, taking our patience and humor along.

Horses display stress in a million ways, including stiff necks, upset digestion, wild eyes, and flattened ears. Eating and drinking habits can change. Horses under stress can be moody, cranky, and irritable. Do you notice any of these symptoms when you look in the mirror?

Dressage has an exercise called a half-halt. Its purpose is to improve the horse's balance and attention. In the best application, it's a near Zen-like experience of beginning fresh.

Maybe a *human* half-halt would help right now—just a pause to catch your balance. You don't have to gallop along with the herd. You can ride your own path.

If you are busy, you could choose to just skip the barn visit. Christmas isn't really their kind of holiday anyway. Horses will wear that stupid Santa hat to please you, but their heart isn't in it. And if your mind is on everything you haven't gotten done, you aren't such great company anyway.

If you do go to the barn, give your ambition a break. This isn't the time to work on cleaning up that canter depart or beginning half-pass work. It's the season to expect less; some days it's an achievement to stand in his stall. There is that warm place under his mane and just resting a hand there is a healing. If you are working on listening—and you should be—then let his cue to you be peace. Breathe. Let be.

If that just isn't enough, your horse wants me to mention that the holidays are a good time for a rider to take up equine massage. Conscious touch is a special kind of groundwork.

If you really want to ride, walking can be plenty. Set the clock to horse time. Let the ride be a slow dance. Let your horse's hips sway you. Resistance melts and warms you from the bottom up. Saunter around until your brain gets soft. Then take a few minutes and remember. Sometimes in the effort to improve and move ahead, we forget to look at the big picture. You have a pony. The rest is decoration.

However you feel about the holidays, they are here. Lit up with all the usual blessings and challenges. And like every other day, you are a rider. You can half-halt, and then do an upward transition—to peace.

A TRAINING JOURNAL, TOLD FROM TWO VIEWPOINTS

If there is an annual pony day, it should be Christmas.

I'm a Dressage Queen with an unlikely soft spot for vertically-challenged horses. Too often they get small patience from humans who treat them with low regard. Or at the very least, these condensed equines are under-estimated—although they are smart, tough, and very athletic. In the last few years that I've been working with a local horse rescue, I've fostered or trained seven or eight diminutives. I mention this because Bhim was not my first mini-rodeo.

***

Bhim's the name. Sanskrit for "Great One." I was running a herd—the North Dakota Fourteen, they called us. Honestly, I'm not wild about humans. They're a confused and emotionally un-balanced bunch. They pretend to like you and then turn on you as soon as they catch you. Don't trust 'em.

***

The North Dakota Fourteen arrived in Colorado looking for homes. They were a neglected herd and a group of local horse rescues stepped up. The horses arrived in a big trailer and there was a day of shots, hoof repair from a farrier, and gelding for the stallions. Bhim won the trifecta on that day and he wasn't happy about it.

***

I tried to teach those humans some respect. It didn't work, but I stood up on my hind legs and fought hard. Humans don't fight fair.

***

Most of the minis got adopted pretty quickly. Eventually Bhim was the only one left. His attitude didn't endear him to potential homes. He arrived at my barn with an un-related mini-mule, who had a halter on full time. Her nose band showed a stripe of hair rubbed to callous and it didn't take a genius to guess why. She was cantankerous and shy. Mules are persnickety about issues like trust. But she was easy compared to Bhim. Six months later she went to a wonderful home. Bhim was still barely catch-able and my progress reports on him were not overly impressive. He was making me look bad, so I doubled down and went even slower.

***

I am very tough and I like to hold a grudge. Here's my backside, I could kick you in the knee, you know. And don't call me cute. I'm a whole lot badder than that!

***

The first while Bhim was here, catching him was the big event. We spent a lot of time sizing each other up. I wanted him to volunteer and he wanted me to go away. The rescue used treats to catch him but he wouldn't even look at me, much less take treats from me. Wouldn't consider it—it was like a treat hunger-strike. So instead, we did the ground-work two-step toward a corner. Eventually he would assume a position that was permission, if not surrender. He allowed me to halter him if I was slow and asked politely. It was an armed truce. It's about then that I found out his tiny ears liked to be scratched. Just his ears.

***

The leadership in this barn could use some help. Clara, the young mare, told me she has been trying to take over since her mom, Windy, died, but no one believes her. Everyone listens to The Grandfather Horse, but he's a relic who moves like a brick. I could tell he needed a leg man. And this donkey won't stop staring at me.

***

The rescue got calls on Bhim. He has eye-catching pinto coloring and more than once I emailed people who were interested and invited them to come. I told the truth. He was proud and smart, a work in progress. And most days I could catch him in ten or fifteen minutes. He was learning to lead, but he still got away from me too often. On top of that he doesn't like kids one tiny bit.

No one asked about him, not one nibble. Finally, one couple came looking for a therapy program they were starting. He was clearly a really bad prospect, but they kept saying he was cute. Bhim was a lot more complicated than "cute," so the answer was no.

***

Okay, I changed my mind about the donkey, Edgar Rice Burro. He's my body guard, he saved me. The human wrote about it and we like to hang out. He's an intelligent Longear, but still, I don't understand his attraction to humans.

***

By now Bhim is tolerating the farrier even when he's sober. He and Edgar give each other moral support for this hell-ish procedure. Sometimes Edgar Rice Burro won't let the farrier near Bhim, so we have to put him in another pen. Then Edgar brays like a siren, mourning their separation, and opens the gates in between them so he can rest his nose on Bhim in solidarity during the hoof trim. Anyone can see it is a love that is true.

***

How did these geldings get along before me? That draft-cross can hardly even find the hay if I don't lead the way. That weird bay horse is pacing less and helping when Edgar and I muck with the human, who does a passable job as long as I keep an eye on her. Sometimes when my ears are itchy, I ask her to scratch them for me. But I act very cool about it and barely whisper my thanks. She gets a bit too enthusiastic, given the chance.

***

Bhim still over-reacts on the lead rope all the time—still quick to spook. Sometimes he lets tall strangers pet him on the head but the short humans are still cause for extreme alarm. It's been fifteen months; I'm a better trainer than this. The thing Bhim does best, with Edgar's help, is steady new horses, show them the barn ways, and negotiate them into the herd. He's a genius, even with mares.

Apparently, the way this training thing works is always different with each horse. You can think you're training one thing and what they learn is something else entirely. You might be so involved in your own amazing training skills, that you might not notice they are working for you in another way entirely. I was confounded, so busy watching a little horse that I missed the big picture.

So, I sent one last training report to Pat at the rescue, "It seems Bhim has made himself indispensable around here." Because that "Pony for Christmas" wish never gets old. Sometimes it comes true for the humans and sometimes for the pony.

THE LAST GOAT STANDING

I've been trying to *not* write about goats all week. I wanted to write something inspiring about art and dressage. I've kind of been being a goat about it, truth be told. Stubborn. Headstrong. Ornery. But I know when I'm out-goated, so I'll tell you about JoeGoat.

First, understand that goats aren't for everyone. You have to be a little bit of a goat to own one. And of course, the term "own" is perhaps an exaggeration. Okay, more of an out-and-out lie.

Goats appropriated my farm the first year I moved here. I got a pair of kids and so did a neighbor, who abandoned her twins within the week—at my farm. I was going to return her pair to the breeder that next weekend. It was just too much work bottle feeding all four of them. Although goats are very friendly and like to untie your shoelaces, their number one rule is to put their own desires first, no matter what, in every situation. It isn't that you can't train them; they just learn what they want.

Then Barney, the neighbor's blond goat, fell into a water trough and almost drowned. He was so contrite when I used the hair dryer on him that I decided he could stay, but JoeGoat, his brown twin, had to go back.

I called ahead and JoeGoat got in the cab of the truck with me. I can't really explain what happened next, but he talked me out of breaking up on the way.

***

You know I'm the worst goat. Comin' from the far left side of contrary. I'm the most unlikable of all the kids. I know you don't like me much, but you probably like me more than anyone else ever would.

***

Unlikeable was an understatement but his logic hit a chord. So, by the time we arrived, I left him in the cab and went in to explain to the breeder. She shook her head, pressed a few free gallons of goat milk on me, and sent us back home.

That was when things changed. JoeGoat went through a period of self-discovery. Not all of us get a message as loud as Joe did and his was undeniable. He confessed that he was not really a goat at all. He was a llama, graceful and curious, who was trapped in the body of a short-necked, stiff-legged goat. And he was mad about it.

But that wasn't the important part. He had fallen in love. Holiday was a young llama back then, with a slightly crooked front tooth and bangs that fell in his eyes. JoeGoat was besotted.

At first, I was naive enough to think that I could keep them separate, but several times a day Joe broke into the llama pen. He'd squeeze himself through a tiny crack or weasel the gate; then I'd wrestle him back in the goat pen and repair the damage.

Then for a while, he was always out, but I couldn't find the leak. The goat pen had wooden cable spools for the goats to play on, so Joe would tip one on its side and roll it to the fence. After setting it upright again, he got on top and launched himself over the fence and in with the llamas. Smart enough.

I gave up the fence fight. Joe Goat abandoned his twin and went to live with Holiday and the other llamas... but it wasn't a happy ending. Joe was a jealous suitor—belligerently monogamous. And for the rest of his life, JoeGoat's love was unrequited. Partly because Joe was a jerk and tried to keep Holiday separate from the other llamas. That and Holiday just wasn't into goats. It didn't matter though; Joe was cross-dressing the dream. But with less hair. Sound familiar?

We lost Joe this week. Just like before, he didn't want to go. We had a rough trip in the truck on icy roads on a foggy, snowy morning. During the thirty-mile, hour-long trip to the vet, he tried to talk me out of it again. He couldn't stand or even hold his head up. His body was in pain; failing him. Even then, he was a stubborn old goat, almost impossible to get along with. That was what I loved about him.

Don't feel too sorry for JoeGoat. He had a great life; for fourteen years, he head-butted the world on his own terms. He lived an *alternate lifestyle* on a liberal farm that had tolerance for narcissistic ruminants. And please, no platitudes. He courted no sympathy before and I can't imagine he wants it now. JoeGoat isn't the Rainbow Bridge sort. My guess is that he's broken out, found the caretakers' picnic area, and jumped on the table and eaten the melon salad. Again.

Now Sumo is the last goat standing—fifteen come spring. He went for a check-up this week. The vet says he has outlived his teeth and they're getting too long. But who am I to judge. I get horse hairs growing out of my chin from time to time.

Why should anyone care about the insignificant lives of two old goats? In the course of the world, our lives aren't any bigger than theirs and JoeGoat is a better teacher than some. If he cared, which he didn't, he would probably have asked if you were getting your way enough. Sometimes you just *should*, you know.

Finally, if you feel a need to remember him someway, which again, he would think was stupid in the first place, perhaps the thing to do every once in a while, is be an obnoxious pain in the butt and insist on it being all about you—at everyone else's inconvenience. Then bleat about it.

(We'll miss you, you old snart.)

WHY I LIKE BAD-DOGS

I wasn't always this way. There was a time when I was a serial Golden Retriever owner. I wanted a life that was sunny and uncomplicated. I mean no offense to any good dogs out there, but one day I got a taste for something a bit more contrary. Goldens started to look like they all had low self-esteem; they were trying entirely too hard to please. Just like Eddie Haskell, you could almost hear them say, "Well, hello Anna, have you lost weight?" *wag-wag-wag*

One day it started sounding just a bit insincere. That was clearly the kind of ungrateful thought that a bad-dog, or some-one who liked bad-dogs, would think. They say people pick dogs that mirror them. No argument from me.

And then Agatha became my dog but she found me only marginally passable company. She was a basset hound who drove all men wild, except the one whose heart she desired the most. Every Monday she patiently looked down the alley, wait-ing for the trash man. Then she would debase herself, flirting in the cheapest, most tawdry way. But she didn't care. Where-ever it was he went, he had all that stinky, rotting garbage with him. She was a dog with a dream and I could respect that.

Disclaimer: I do have one not-quite-bad-dog now. Or maybe she just seems that way because she's smarter and uses telepathy on the rest of us. Her name is Tomboy—she's not very feminine. She's more the strong, silent type.

***

Just Tom is fine. And spare me the pink bow. I've got work to do.

***

She and I share a cult of two hearts and there is no greater compliment to pay a dog. Tommi had her twelfth birthday this week. She's always been a wild child, but now she's too old to bring half-dead bunnies into the house anymore, although she does bag a tumbleweed every now and then. How you can tell she's a good dog is that she hasn't killed any Corgis yet. Old dogs are not required to be polite to screaming toddlers or Corgis. It's common knowledge.

Agatha was the first in a long line of spectacular bad-dogs, but not the last. There were a couple of tough cattle dogs, Spam and Hero, who moved to the farm with me, and my big Briard boy, Howdy. I miss them every day, but I honor their memory by welcoming more bad-dogs to our home.

That's how Walter and Preacher Man got here.

I would like to say the little Corgi men are great barn dogs. It wouldn't be true. When Walter comes to the barn, he considers himself a world-class mucker. But there are crucial steps in the process that he leaves out and when I call him out of a stall, he is gasping, chewing, and licking with the effort.

Want an up-date on his health? Walter continues to have a total disregard for his terminal prognosis.

***

Those vet-women. They hand out treats like there's no tomorrow. Get it?

***

It's a Corgi dream of a harem. His symptoms are steady, but he's picking fights so everyone will know what a big bad-dog he is. He's outlived his "expiration date" by six months, but science is boring, the ducks need some order in their lives, and there is barking to be done. Get over it.

A year later, Preacher Man arrived at the airport, leaving a trail of broken hearts and eardrums in Texas. Preacher is more of a free-thinker.

***

Being house-broken is for saps. Mark it mine! Preacher was here.

***

Preacher Man has never made it to the barn. If he gets out of the backyard with the other dogs, he bolts straight down the driveway, across the road and over the far horizon. He has wanderlust. And a leash on now, which limits his mucking ability.

But they mostly prefer their inside job of waiting under my desk when I write, like sleeping sharks. They love my writing, of course, but sometimes I drop my lunch. I've learned that the secret to living with screaming alarms, day and night, is to not be alarmed.

To be honest, when I was younger I was a lost dog myself. I desperately needed that unconditional Golden love for a while. Years later, I found my voice and I barked like Preacher. To love a bad-dog is to celebrate love in the form of chaos. It's every bit as unconditional, just a bit more open to the uncontrollable. It means living in a place of constant forgiveness. Another word for that is rescue.

And now there are days when Preacher is able to sit quietly meditating, draped over my lap like a wet towel. He is soft and manages just a few sighs and moans, which is almost like being quiet… and I see a Corgi version of that look Agatha gave the trash man thirty years ago.

Dogs. Bless their big fat hearts. I'd be a mangy stray without them.

THE LONG GOODBYE: VINNIE

It makes perfect sense to tell the story of an off-the-track Thoroughbred in the midst of the Triple Crown frenzy. Some of us love racing and some can't stand to watch, but we all agree on one truth: Thoroughbred horses are bold, athletic, and bursting with heart.

Is there a foal born who doesn't arrive with a human's dream attached? They're all legs and big ears, galloping to keep up with Mom's slow trot, while Fogelberg's *Run for the Roses* swells to a crescendo. We've seen the promos before the race. The foal stops and the camera zooms in close to his big, soft eye. His intelligence is undeniable.

Trigger warning: Real life.

On the day that Vinnie was born, someone looked at him with awe. We don't know who, or where. We can't trace him that far back—the tattoo inside his lip isn't readable. But he said goodbye to his family and landed at Thistledown Racino, a combination Thoroughbred race track and casino in North Randall, Ohio, on the outskirts of Cleveland. Do you know the place? The track has declined in recent years because it doesn't have newer slot machines like the neighboring tracks.

We don't know for sure if he raced but when Vinnie was no longer useful at the track, his owners listed him with CANTER (The Communication Alliance to Network Thoroughbred Ex-Racehorses) in Ohio. He was not a rescue, but listed for sale. Another horse from the same owner was purchased by a

Colorado trainer, with one catch. It was a two-for-one deal; if the trainer wanted the chestnut she liked, then the bay, Vinnie, had to go along in the deal. No charge.

I doubt it was a sad farewell or a warm welcome to Colorado. Clearly Vinnie was no prize. At some point around this time, someone mentioned a diagnosis of Shivers, a degenerative neurological disease with no cure. We don't know who diagnosed it or much else about him during this time. He must have had some training.

The Colorado trainer soon "donated" him on to a rather elite private riding program. He's been there the last eight years, jumping mostly. It's a challenge for a horse to work in a program where riders change almost daily. It's safe to say his riders weren't necessarily the best but he took good care of them for the next few years. We hear all the girls loved him.

But then Vinnie started to unravel. We were told differing stories about this part, too. He just "decided" not to get in the trailer one day. He flipped over in trailers. He needed to be tranquilized for the farrier. He only hated the nail hammering part of farrier work. He had horrible separation anxiety. He didn't like being tied. The list goes on, but he got booted out of the riding program and spent all winter in pasture with no supplemental feed. He got thin. Then the order came down; Vinnie was no longer paying his way and he needed to move on. Right away. One more time.

You know the next part: somebody called somebody and word got to a person with a soft spot for off the track Thoroughbreds. She and a friend decided to sponsor Vinnie, with help from a local rescue, and I agreed he could come to my farm.

I went to see him with one of his sponsors-to-be. We had low expectations, and even if he was worse than we expected, we knew we'd still want him. He was in desperate circumstances so there wasn't much doubt. When we arrived, he was alone in an arena with a horse trailer. He was skinny and so filled with anxiety that he seemed distracted and antsy—kind of slow-motion frantic. He was moving badly behind, so skinny that his withers had a pointy peak, but his eye was soft. He had some idea he might be applying for a job and first impressions probably mattered, but he was a mess with his stomach sucked up and a dusty dullness to his coat.

We walked to the trailer and his hay was inside, just beyond his reach. He paced back and forth—tense with hunger. His backbone was visible and he had a way of tucking his butt under himself to compensate for whatever was hurting him. At the same time, he was very kind, happy to breathe with me, and match my strides walking until he found a stray bit of manure. He stopped to eat it and now that I looked, there wasn't another visible scrap of manure in the arena. They said he ate all his hay three times a day but I wondered. Maybe Vinnie was lying but I doubt it. Either way, withholding feed is a ridiculous and cruel training technique. I pulled his hay a few feet outside the trailer and he didn't lift his head until it was gone. How many people have failed this horse in his life.

He's a tall lanky gelding, more insecure than shy. He doesn't ask for much. Vinnie's calm with a Cary Grant kind of charm. He kept his head low, level with mine, more accepting than desperate. I let him know he'd be at my barn the next day.

The riding program was afraid we'd get hurt hauling him, so they insisted on delivering him and we spent twenty-four hours hoping Vinnie would survive the trip. The next afternoon when the trailer pulled in, I had a spot ready for him with fresh water and too much hay. I watched him, while he watched me, through the slats as the trailer pulled around. When the door opened, he paused there like a returning war hero. He slowly stepped off the trailer with dignity and calm. The cowboy who hauled him said he walked right in the trailer, no fuss.

Don't go all bliss-ninny on me. I know you want to read a happy rescue story here—only half as much as I want to write one. But that isn't true yet. He's here for two months for evaluation. This is not his happy ending, just a stopover. But Vinnie thinks today is good. He likes the company and they put the hay crazy-close. You can eat all day long.

Vinnie has an odd stride and some nervous affectations. He went on ulcer treatment immediately. We wondered about the Shivers, along with tucked hip, so his sponsors called in a favor with a vet/chiropractor/acupuncturist. Vinnie had needles in his back in a blink. The good news was that she didn't diagnose Shivers. On the down side, she thinks he may have sustained a serious sacroiliac joint injury or even a broken pelvis at some time in the past.

Those words hung in the air for a moment. When? Did it happen at the track? Is that why he was shuffled off for free? Had he been carrying kids over jumps this way? Just then a friend at my barn said Vinnie looked very familiar. She texted me the next day to say he'd been offered to the equine therapy center where she works. That was three years earlier. She'd turned him down back then because he was lame and skinny. In rescue stories, the details never quite add up.

We don't know the end of this story. He has a couple of sponsored months here, so he can be evaluated. He'll be getting plenty to eat, more vet visits, and some supplements and medications to help his back loosen. I'll work with him on confidence and trailer loading. We don't know if he will able to be ridden lightly or not, but we want to give him some time with that part of the evaluation. They told us he was twelve, but his papers say he's fourteen. Vinnie is at the far side of midlife.

Ultimately horses, sometimes even rescue horses, get judged by whether or not they can put in more work. They're valued for what they have to contribute to humans; they still have to prove their monetary worth.

But the really sad part is that even now Vinnie would try again. No matter how many times he's been dismissed, no matter how many goodbyes have come before; he will keep his big Thoroughbred heart open to humans. This horse humbles me. He doesn't have the good sense to quit us. Like his brothers at the track, he will try until his heart bursts.

So, if goodbye is not in your vocabulary, and if you think a heart the size of his will fit inside your barn, then kindly consider adopting a good horse from rescue. Because a *forever home* means more to some of us than others.

THE GRANDFATHER HORSE, NOT DEAD YET

I haven't written about the Grandfather Horse in over a year. Most of that time, I was scared half-to-death and the rest of the time, I was laughing too hard.

I know I'm supposed to credit whatever equine skills I might have to my trainers (I worked with the best), and the famous clinicians I rode with (they were famous for all the right reasons), but when the scabs all healed, my greatest mentor was Spirit, a six-hundred-dollar spotted colt. He has done it all. Twice. And with me on his back. That last part was hard.

No one taught me more about wet T-shirt contests and unplanned vaulting. About reining and dressage. About how to be a horse. He quite simply taught me everything worth knowing. I don't believe in soul-mates, but if I did, the Grandfather Horse is mine. I doubt anyone who knows us would disagree.

***

My human. She tends to exaggerate. I'm just a horse.

***

I'd like to say Spirit, retired to the respected place of Grandfather Horse in our herd, was such a good teacher because he was easy

214

to understand. Nothing could be further from the truth. He was a challenge to ride: quirky, emotional, not particularly athletic, and with a little too much try. (As a trainer, when clients tell me who their horse is, in my mind I switch the pronouns—what she says about her horse is true about herself. Probably true in my case, too.)

These last twelve years of forced retirement have been sheer hell for both of us. Watching him slowly deconstruct with old age has taken more courage than anything I ever did in the saddle.

We had a decrepit routine. He shuffled along, baby-stepping with his eyes perpetually teary and sunken. I learned to schedule his Annual Emergency Sheath Cleaning. The first time, I thought he was dying. Now I mark *Old Man Smegma* on the calendar. The vet probably has a less descriptive name for it.

There was chronic diarrhea and the tendons in his front legs that gave way to bent knees a decade ago. His arthritis was audible. As much as he loved a roll in the sand, he did it rarely. Neither of us thought he would make it back up. I tried being stoic like him. He was holding his own, the best he could, but he lacked his usual humor. Maybe he didn't recognize himself. I notice at this age, I don't.

It changed last spring. He held a good weight all winter and come February, his weight plummeted. He didn't eat differently, but he developed a decidedly bovine appearance. He had thigh gap, significantly less cool in horses. His back dropped even more; he barely had a memory of muscle. It happened so abruptly that I thought I was losing him. It was obvious enough that people mentioned it to me, with a euthanizing look in their eyes. Like I didn't know all his contemporaries were gone already.

So, I called the vet and did blood tests, stirred everything up from diet to turnout partners, and even broke a couple of my own rules. I scrutinized everything every day, and against all odds, the weight came back. It felt like a slow-motion miracle of biblical proportions.

Sometimes he trotted a few strides to his dinner when he came in at night. Then the first real sign of change: He started flicking his tail again. It's his go-to sign of impatience and frustration. I cackled like an old red hen—he felt good enough to behave badly for the first time in years.

He's laying down again. It sounds like two thousand books falling off a table and I flinch to see it, but he's rolling and sunbathing again.

All horses, no matter how good they are, have a tragic flaw—that rude love of a bad habit. When he was younger, Spirit liked to bolt when the halter came off for turnout. A split-second lapse of focus and you could simultaneously get your toes crushed and an arm dislocated. Zero to sixty in a joyous rocket launch. It's slower now, but happening again! On especially fine days, he even spooks sideways.

My Christmas present? I heard hooves pounding, and when I got to the pasture, the Grandfather Horse was running the younger ones ragged. He was flashing his tail and galloping along like a box of rocks.

He just seems to feel stronger. My friend who has the oldest horse I know says at a point her mare's joints fused a bit and the arthritis hurt less. I think my Grandfather Horse may have lived long enough for this special senior discount. Either way, he's got a second wind and he thinks aging gracefully is the worst kind of lame.

The Grandfather Horse is happy again, and I'm like the teacher's pet jumps in the chair, hoping to be picked to answer.

***

I'm a horse of few words, but the old girl's excitable. I was right to pick her, just the same.

***

He's had decades to get used to my awkward ways, he knows I catch up eventually. So, he's sterling in the moonlight. He shows me how to feel the afternoon sun in a whole new way. He's born-again beautiful; it's irresistibly bittersweet.

This week we lost a beloved barn member and when the dead animal transport people came, they gave *me* a senior discount to pick up this senior carcass. I paused a moment… was it a bad joke? Or perhaps an ironic call to arms?

My Grandfather Horse and I, we're still not the most graceful pair, but world, beware! It's sixteen days till Daylight Savings time and almost spring. New grass is on the way. There's a good chance we'll plan a spring breakout—just the two of us.

***

We've got nothing to lose and we're not dead yet.

***

WALTER ON POSITIVE TRAINING FOR VETERINARIANS

Thanks for not mentioning my big nasty scab. I woke up last week with a Corgi toenail inside my ear. It was attached to a Corgi...running in mid-air... trying to find traction...in a fight with a sleeping Briard...next to me on the bed...at about two am. The Briard and I were totally disoriented by the attack. She's getting older and she doesn't wake up limber or alert. Neither do I. There was a lot of flailing and moaning. The aforementioned Corgi, Walter, continued barking frantically while still airborne, and then Preacher Man, who always absolutely loves the sound of his own voice, joined in. Night terrors.

***

Coyotes! Those weird dogs are here! Coyotes!

***

Things have been a little rough in here at the Less-Than-Peaceable-Kingdom the last few months. It's Walter, who has a terminal diagnosis that he couldn't care less about. Hold on, I'm getting to the positive training part.

Walter is great. He never wants anyone's sympathy—not

while the ducks are pooping just on the other side of the fence. Lately I can tell things are sliding for him. He's a little more frantic all the time. The whites of his eyes show too much, like someone pretending enthusiasm about math. Even his tongue has anxiety. And he naps too much. He picks fights with all the dogs. Not the cats—he isn't stupid—but he fights with his friends. We all know it isn't who he is, but it's the way he can let us know he's lost confidence.

It's not his fault. Part of positive training is making sure the dog (or usually in my case, horse) is physically well. Walter isn't. Period. So, we mitigate when we can, keeping him separate but not alone. He always gets the best spot on the sofa, between me and the Dude Rancher, on pizza night.

It's been twenty months since his diagnosis—meaning twenty trips back to the vet. In the beginning, it was the worst thing. He clung to me, pleading with a nervous twitch.

***

Don't let them kill me. They have hot pointy things. You won't be able to live with the guilt. Look at my ears.

***

Because every visit includes a blood draw. A needle for him and several for me—his toenails impaling my arm. As my good vet took him back, he gave me that look. You know the one—warning me that I'd be really sorry if he died right now. He got treats all through the needle process. Then he returned to my lap, pathetically clinging and desperately frightened. Sometimes he would close his eyes and pretend paralysis while we talked about the test results.

***

They've killed me.

***

I hear Corgis have a bit of a reputation with vets sometimes. Selling the notion of positive training is much more challenging when needles are involved. But each month we ween back to check his meds. The plan starts at home: The good thing about taking all those pills is that it takes a good-sized wad of patè— and by patè I mean canned hepatic dog food—to hold them all together. I use twice what's needed.

Walter has outlived his prognosis by almost a year so far. He thinks only suckers believe that stuff in the first place. Walter doesn't actually like car travel, especially the rumble strips, but he loves being an only dog, even if it's just in the car. He's a complicated guy that way. When we pull up to the vet's, he peers over the dash with a sly smile. This last trip in, the women at the front desk pulled out the treat jar as soon as he came through the door. He is barely tall enough to see over the edge, but he stands up and they oblige him handfuls of treats just for coming in.

***

These vet-women are so trainable; they turn to mush when they see me. I'm the Dog, all right.

***

As long as he stood there, the treats kept coming. By the time he got on the scale, he was up a few ounces. We fight to keep weight on him, but I knew this weight gain was all extremely recent. I offered to pay a treat surcharge since they use the smelly moist liver kind. Then Walter and I waddle back to the exam room and settle. He can't take his eyes off the door.

***

Where is she? Will she come soon? She's taking forever.

***

She greets us and they leave for the blood draw. Later the tests confirm what his recent behavior shows. His numbers are worse than ever but he loves her anyway.

My vet is a genius—I know her good work has given us this precious time. It's a fair-sized practice, with several perfect employees who all seem to know Walter. When the patient comes first it shows. Meaning Walter caught on after a couple of visits and then it was full steam ahead.

Now I can't remember who used positive reinforcement in the beginning, but that's how the magic works. It doesn't matter who starts it; it becomes a habit and pretty soon we're all smacking our lips and singing *Give Peace a Chance*. It's not just a training method, it's a lifestyle.

There's so much that's out of our control in this world. You never know what tomorrow will bring. It could take you a while to find your forever home, only to find out… well, just thinking about it all could get you down. But life's too short to spend pouting in detention. Better to have a party and get to be smart all the time.

***

Dance the Good Boy dance and teach them to reward you every moment. Now enough of this bliss-ninny chatter, I think I hear treats coming.

***

HOW MUCH LONGER DO YOU THINK YOU CAN DO THIS?

"How much longer do you think you can do this?"

This week I received a request from a reader, my age, sixty. She's frustrated at being asked that question repeatedly. The reader's friend advises that my reader and her husband "should get rid of over thirty equines and their farm and all the work, and buy a motor-home and travel and 'have some fun' for a change!"

Her friend is asking her when she's going to grow out of her horse phase. *Isn't that cute?*

I guess I can understand the question. Some of my family retired to the Snowbird lifestyle. Most were farmers who dreamed of retirement. My parents resided in Space 924 in a Mesa, Arizona, trailer park and they loved the lifestyle back in the day. When I visited them, I couldn't help but wonder, "How much longer do you think you can do this?"

It should be common knowledge; work is in the eye of the beholder. Sometimes visitors to my farm start by saying it looks like a lot of work. I used to kind of survey the place with them, trying to see what they were looking at. I get a bit literal from time to time. In the end, our biggest passions are usually a lot of work, if you think to use that word. Anything can be work (or play) if you call it that. Some of us think mucking on a fine day with a semi-well-intentioned long-ear to help is about as much fun as anyone is due.

I am going to be truthful; there are things I have stopped doing. I don't start young horses anymore. My herd depends on me. I'm proof that at a certain age, at least some of us grow some common sense, but it's only because my life is so precious to me now. I've also recently worked with some of the most challenging horses I've ever known recently—horses whose complexity would have evaded me when I was younger. It's a trade-off.

I notice retirement, or even vacations, work best when the place you travel to is better than your day-to-day life at home. For lots of us who have made our home-barn a haven, travel loses its appeal. Especially if our friends are grazers, instead of card players.

Dear Reader, in a tone reminiscent of your mother, "I'm worried about the friends you spend time with, Honey."

Can I tell you about my new friends? Last fall, here in Colorado there was a horrible horse abuse case. Many concerned horse owners showed up at a town-hall meeting with authorities to talk about what could be done.

I planned on going early but got distracted and lost time mucking. When I looked at my watch, I bolted into the house, changed out of my pajamas, and slapped a cap on my head. I arrived just in time and once the session was open to questions, I stood in line at the microphone. It was a long line—we all had something to say.

From that vantage point I looked around the room and saw many *women of a certain age.* They wore jeans and frankly, everybody's hair looked about like mine. We wore sturdy shoes and were women of passion. We talked with conviction about horse welfare, to people who were younger than us and held positions of power in the county government. It was a sunny day; when we were younger we might have gone riding instead of standing up and insisting that reporting horse abuse be taken more seriously. But then, *women of a certain age* have had more time with horses; we have more to be grateful for.

This week that abuse case was in court. Although there was

international outrage over this case, although thousands of people voiced concern, there were only a handful of us who came to court most days. We were *women of a certain age*. We wiggled in our seats uncomfortably, through hours of testimony. Our backs got stiff, not from throwing hay and moving bags of grain, but by sitting still with no sunlight. Our backs got stiff from what we were hearing and seeing.

But we weren't there because we're old and have nothing better to do with our time. We work, our time is valuable, but we've also learned to prioritize time into freedom. We owe a debt to the horses in our lives; we'll keep doing what we do.

At the end of the court day, we didn't linger, chatting over drinks. We rushed home to decompress in our barns. We looked at our old horses, our rescues, our good working horses, and made the promise again—*Never!* As we picked up muck forks, our breathing slowed and angry shoulders started to release. There's some sort of universal balance struck between human emotional excrement and the actual muck created by horses.

Dear Reader, I thought I would write a witty call to arms for us gray mares. It didn't turn out that way. You said you do hoof work, rehabilitating and rescuing horses. You are a *woman of a certain age* so I'm not telling you anything new. But I've seen way too many nasty photos this week in court and my humor has gone flat. I'll answer the question.

"How much longer do you think you can do this?"

I pray that we never give up thinking we can do this. Or any other thing that our conscience says needs doing. And eventually, when they pry that muck fork out of our cold, dead hands, we go to a place where our horses graze in knee-high grass and no one questions our intentions or abilities.

THE THING ABOUT HORSES AND HEALING: VINNIE

We see them from the road standing with heads low, often alone. So, we slow down and use phones to take photos. We keep a legal distance but most of us have seen neglected horses and reported them to authorities… or been haunted, wishing we had. The photos are long distance and slightly out of focus, but it's easy to see ribs showing and they might be lame to the eye when moving. You know the horse is in trouble.

But I'm looking at another photo now. What's with the pudgy bay in a fly mask? Consider it his photo from the Rescue Relocation Program. It's Vinnie, here for evaluation. I like this photo of him, blurriness and all, at the far corner of the pasture, grazing with a fly mask with one ear torn off. It's hard to see but there's a bird perched on those pointy withers of his. Oh, and it's hard to see his ribs now, too. This is his "after" picture. Time has passed since I first wrote about Vinnie and here's an update.

Vinnie's swell. He is more socially interactive now. It took over a week, but he started lying down in the sun eventually. I wasn't sure he could. He's up to date with vaccines and he's received a series of Pentosan injections for those stiff joints. He stands quietly while I give shots; they've been nothing short of a miracle for Vinnie. Now he gallops for fun; he comes at a run when I call him in. His stride is wildly long and joyous.

When he arrived, it was just the opposite. And we still doubt he will be ride-able with an old injury that means his hind end looks like an egg beater from time to time. But his heart is big and full, he loves being scratched, and it looks like he is headed to foster later this month and hopefully a forever home soon. Yay, Vinnie.

It's good news, isn't it? We love these stories and part of it is selfish. Vinnie heals us all a little bit when we hear about him. It's the crazy thing about horses. I've had a couple of occasions when it was my job to ask people for money for horse advocacy and rescue. I don't play fair; I ask the tough question first:

"How many of you have been rescued by a horse?"

Then I watch. Invariably most hands quickly go up, with easy smiles and some laughter. Some of us were rescued from being cosmetic zombies, tech junkies, or victims of fashion. We're saved from boredom and complacency. We use horses as an excuse to be outside in the sun instead of cleaning the house. Each of us has a way of describing that irresistible smell that's part sweat, part fly spray, and part dream-come-true.

But as I look around the group, some jaws are set and their eyes seem distant, hidden under furrowed brows. They straighten their shoulders a bit but there is no smile. They raise their hands resolutely and hold them high and still—as if testifying; as if standing to be counted. For them, rescue is a life-and-death personal issue. I recognize these committed hands because I raise mine the exact same way. In that moment, we lose our humor because the depth of gratitude we feel toward horses overwhelms us. We literally owe our presence in the world to the memory of some old horse.

About then my voice seizes up. I don't want this to be about me because there are so many others with the same experience. I'm common in this group. So, I continue to ask for money and notice quite a few of us have something in our eye. We act like its dust because we've developed some pride, but we're fooling no one.

And so, when we see a photo of Vinnie like this, even as we

celebrate him, we see ourselves. That's how rescue works—it's contagious. It doesn't matter who does it first, horse or human, but it starts in a small, seemingly insignificant way and eventually radiates out in all directions. In the beginning, it's rough. Horses reflect our fear and hurt, but if we ride it out, smelling mane and trying to forge a language with a horse, in the end we reflect their confidence. We become good lead mares in our own lives.

"Riding is a school of humility and selflessness, its practice if it is done well, tends to make better Human Beings" —Nuno Oliveira

We started young. Lots of us came to positive horsemanship because of rough handling as children. We learned firsthand that violent dominance never builds trust, and lots of us escaped to the barn. Horses were the safe haven we found there. They spoke the language we had hoped to hear in our homes.

Horse-people are prone to say that horses are cheaper than therapy. I have done the research and it isn't actually true. But the more time we spend with horses, the more we heal. As we move forward with our horses, it gets easier to let go of fear in our human lives and forgive ourselves of our pasts. For some of us, being with a horse is our first taste of honesty. It works like church because even the staunchest atheist can see the divinity in a horse. They're undeniable miracles and some of it rubs off on us. Like salvation.

The thing about horses rescuing us is that it works impersonally, as consistent as gravity, healing each of us whether we think we need it or not. We just say yes, and whether we need a healing from helmet hair or total abandonment in the world, horses will carry us through it. When the day comes that we realize the debt we owe to horses, we work to do better for them. We learn to ride more kindly and communicate more clearly. We discover we have compassion to spare, so we give back by helping other horses.

For some of us, horses are just a "hobby," an overwhelming

passion that drives our lifestyle, finances, and everyday choices and activities. It's like having a combination gambling addiction and an obsessive-compulsive disorder, which we proudly brag about, while spending every spare moment, year after year, in the company of horses.

And then for a lot of us, it's something bigger than that.

BUYING THE RIGHT TO MAKE A CORRECTION

She's as tough and smart a dog as I've ever known. Her name's Tomboy. I don't write about her often enough; she's a little more serious than my Corgi men. She's a Briard, a French herding breed that has a very protective side. Tomboy appointed herself my personal bodyguard when she was a tiny pup and has done a flawless job of guarding and herding me every day of her life. Her commitment is fierce.

On that particular day, I was having a party on the farm. There were lots of dogs running around and Tomboy broke up a few slight dog altercations but mainly she had my back. Literally. Relentlessly. Then the guy on the motorcycle arrived.

The guy was dating a friend and we all welcomed him because of her. I'd met him and his dogs previously. He made sure everyone knew he was a man of great spiritual faith. He had two yellow labs and every time he came close, they both hit the ground and rolled belly up. They were fearful, and I took their opinion into account as well.

He parked his bike and walked toward me, and quietly, Tomboy moved from behind me to block his path. She just put herself between us; no growl, just watching. The guy took a step to go around her but she moved to keep her position. Then he told her to lie down, but she stuck to her spot. He said something I didn't entirely hear, while smiling at me, and it dawned on me that he was going to roll her.

Wikipedia's explanation: "An alpha roll is a technique used in dog training to discipline a misbehaving dog. It consists of flipping the dog onto its back and holding it in that position, sometimes by the throat. The theory is that this teaches the dog that the trainer is the pack leader (or alpha animal)."

Rolling a dog is a controversial technique, but in our case, it was black-and-white wrong. She wasn't disobedient; she just didn't trust him. She's always been a good judge of character so I believed her. But he had no right to punish her in the first place, so I got between the guy and Tomboy, because I have her back, too. I asked him to stop. He started to explain to me what he was doing was helping me train my dog. I said, "She's doing her job just fine." I thought about his dogs and stood my ground. "Back off."

Like most of us, my charming hostess act only goes so far. And this guy was an arrogant jerk, but we commonly see riders like this in the horse world. They confuse leadership with belligerence. And yes, professionals do it as well. The belief is that if we show weakness the war is lost and the animal will be spoiled. It's Neanderthal thinking. Worst of all, it negates the horse's intelligence as well. Lots of us were taught this method when we started with horses. I certainly was.

It's obvious that this guy had no right to correct Tomboy, but when *do* we have the right? Even with our own horses and dogs, when is the most effective time? And when are we taking their behaviors too personally and missing the message?

First, if you are embarrassed or frustrated or mad, just take a break. Emotions are selfish; they're all about you. I'm always surprised when people think that their horse has a vendetta against them, when the simple truth is that behavior isn't personal. Is your ego offended? Is your animal healthy? Is he hungry? Set him up to succeed by making sure he is ready to learn.

Animals can't learn if they are afraid—obvious and simple. It's the reason we harp on about relaxation in dressage. Sure, they can learn fear and distrust; the guy's labs were proof of that. If we walk into a pen like a cave man with a club, we've lost already. We have to define ourselves as a leader, yes, but someone who inspires confidence and safety. In other words, we have to evolve out of the old model if we want a better response.

On any given day, I believe we have to *buy the right* to correct a horse. How else could it be meaningful? It can be as simple as asking for his eye or acknowledging a calming signal. Especially with our own horses, pause and let them volunteer. Don't hurry them or do it for them. Allow them to participate by coming to you or lowering their heads—engage them. If catching is an issue, then that's the place to start healing old experiences. If your horse acts like you're a predator, listen and take the cue. It's the only place to begin.

Never underestimate the power of touch. Current research says that horses prefer a scratch to a pat as a reward, but I think they actually prefer a flat hand lying still. Connection with a horse is as simple as touch and as intimate as breath. It's enough.

Then ask for his best work by communicating with subtle clarity. Consistently. It sounds idiotically simple but each time we cue an animal, we're either training response or resistance. Energy or dullness. If you don't like what your horse reflects back to you, take him at his word, and negotiate with the new information. See yourself as intelligent.

The positive model of training has lots of gray area. If the horse is spooked and distracted, he won't always hear you whisper. Sometimes you might need to raise your energy to get his attention. The art is to be able to adjust your cues bigger or smaller, without emotion. If you must be loud, do it just once, and then get immediately quiet and find a way to say *good boy* in the next minute. You want the first thing he hears to be a reward. Be generous, work toward a tendency of patience, and then when you make the inevitable mistakes, he will show you that tolerance as well.

Finally, humor me with one more remembrance of Tomboy. I was having a sick day, lying on the couch dozing. She slowly climbed up and gently reclined on my chest. Her torso was as long as mine, so her head was just below my chin. She was perfectly still; breathing with me. The hair that normally covered her face had fallen to the side and I could see her eye, unblinking and deep, staring into mine. When I woke up again, she hadn't moved. It's a small moment, but I'm not sure she'd even blinked. She held vigil, warming my body, and literally keeping an eye on me while I was weak. It was healing to feel so protected.

Loyalty and partnership are words to value and always the goal with our animals—but we can't demand them or coax them with cookies. They're a gift, given freely, in exchange for respect.

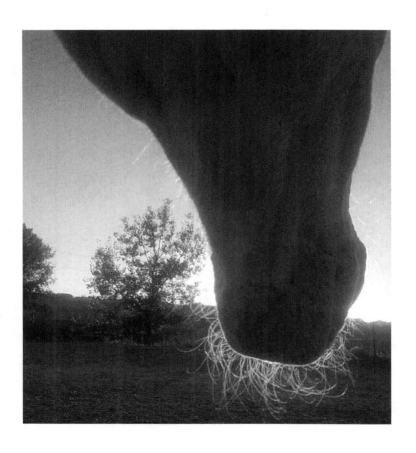

CARE-GIVING AND THE ART OF MUCKING

We have a shade tree next to the barn runs that gives the sweetest summer shade, but wreaks havoc on winter footing. Colorado temps frequently take forty-degree mood swings in a few hours. Fresh muck can land in wet spring snow and a brief moment later, freeze so solid that a pick ax would be useless. But a few hours after that, the muck has dissolved and is indistinguishable from the mud underneath. Then I do some environmental engineering; shoveling this different quality of muck and trenching small puddles into bigger puddles to drain, only to have that pudding-mess freeze into a skating rink in each run again.

It makes the walk to turn-out a cautious process each morning. A fall on ice hurts me more than an unplanned dismount at my age, and the horses know they can't trust the ground and are just as nervous as me. The Grandfather Horse is the most worried, so as he takes one slow skate of a step at a time. I'm his care-giver; it's my pleasure to go his speed.

There's plenty of time to wax nostalgic as we dodder our way to turnout. Back when he was a hot-rod four-year-old, just at this time in the spring, we found him in his turnout pen barely able to stand. His hind-half had lost all coordination; he could barely balance upright. We got him to stagger inside and called the emergency vet. Naturally, I feared a damaged spine or something neurological. The vet's best guess was that my horse had taken a fall, done the splits behind, and somehow torn his inner thigh muscles. He came away with pain killer, six weeks of stall rest, and I was ecstatic with the nebulous explanation.

I drove out to see him every day—this was before Infinity Farm—and massaged mineral ice on his torn muscles, resting my cheek on his rump next to his tail and watching his eyes go soft, as I braved rude jokes from my barn friends. Embarrassment is part of the care-giver gig. It's for better or worse, and if you do your utmost and are lucky, you get to keep your job as they become old and frail. The reward is this dawdling walk.

And in some crazy way, more years of mucking feels like a reward to most of us. We don't understand how others can look out the window and feel nothing as winds chill arthritic bones of horses without shelter or dogs who live on chains.

The upside of spring mucking is that it's also itch season in the barn. So, a curry stays in the muck cart and there are some sweet shedding moments with the herd, even if it makes the job take twice as long. These slow, hairy hours are the very best. I could afford to hire-out my mucking but in the end, I always know I'd miss it too much.

It isn't that care-givers love manure, but it's part of the package. Horses understand the law of reciprocity as well as we do, and we strive for integrity with each other. It's an economy of give and take. We can't control the world, but we have a balance in our herd.

It isn't truly giving if you keep score, so I've lost count of how many times I've bandaged his injuries or worn out muck forks poking at manure-cicles or felt such magic dancing beneath my saddle that, when my eyes close, I notice I'm filled with light. I believe that these acts are all interchangeable, and I get back so much more than I give.

Sometimes when new people come visit here, it is painfully obvious that this farm is not their dream. I appreciate their honesty. I'm not nuts, I don't just love frolicking on frozen toes in ground blizzards but I notice that the less I can tell the difference between work and play, the stronger I am. Through good days and bad days, there's an overall tendency of sweetness. It's just the simple truth that we all share a very small life here and try to do our best for each other.

There is an art to being a care-giver. Not everyone has the patience for it. You have to want to be there fully, grateful for every stride, rewarding every pause for confidence, holding faith in every conscious choice made together.

In other words, the care used on the ground with an elder walking on ice, is the exact same care we use in the saddle, never letting our hands forget that we are blessed to be with these precious, sentient creatures. Amazed at our luck, we take special care, mold it with good intention, and give it back in the purest form we can.

So, for as long as there is something that needs mucking, we'll keep hold of our forks. Because the world is filled with spite and ego and indifference; people do unconscionable things, leaving others to pay for their shortcomings. But we still have a voice. Even if we are no more than the sum of our intent, each time a whiskery muzzle reaches toward a hand, it's undeniable that for that moment, a small act changed the whole world.

ON BEING AN OLD GRAY MARE WITH CHRONIC LAMENESS

It's a shooting pain. Usually my foot is brick-tight and I can't bend my toes. When I do manage to bend them in a natural walking angle, there's a big red pain. I think my toes have cracked off my foot and it feels wet—like hot acid-blood is filling my boot. But I'm trying to be stoic, like my Grandfather Horse.

My lameness started slow and small, ten years ago. Sometimes it felt like I had sprained a toe, but eventually I got orthotics. They worked like therapeutic shoeing does for a horse, and things were fine if I didn't teach an all-day clinic or get stepped on.

Then last year my left foot started to get wider. And thicker. I attempted to a veterinary diagnosis in the shower. At first I worried that I was foundering, but no, this is only one foot and it felt more like a coffin bone coming through the bottom. Could it be navicular? Then I asked Edgar Rice Burro's opinion.

By the last lesson of the day, my foot was swollen so badly that my boot fit like a corset. But that might not be a bad thing, right? Probably navicular; is there a human generic for *Isoxophrine*?

Ack. I've become one of *those* women.

The more it hurts, the more I respect my Grandfather Horse, retired for more than a decade now with suspensory tendon damage and arthritis. There is no spring to his step. I used to walk him slowly and feel like I was being so kind to the doddering old gelding. Now we're moving about even.

None of my shoes fit. Well, it's just one shoe in each pair that doesn't fit. My crocs still fit—which isn't a big loss of style for me. Finally, I think about doing the unthinkable. But I wouldn't want to rush to any conclusions... so I just think about it another year or so. Eventually I cross the line. I call the doctor. In my mind, I try to think of him as a farrier. I like my farrier.

As the nurse takes me down the hall to the exam room, my limp echoes in the same way it does when a lame horse moves on pavement. Of course, I compare it all to a lameness check; I understand those. So, when they take the x-rays, I think of the horses I've held and how convenient this human set-up would be for my vet.

Then I'm staring at my foot from the exam chair when the doctor bursts in, says hello, and immediately starts dissecting the print-out of the x-ray. He doesn't explain much about the problem, but the x-ray is obvious enough. Instead he's madly scribbling, drawing cut lines, and enthusiastically planning the grisly parts, just the way I plan a training path for a troubled horse. Iffy bedside manner, but he seems to enjoy his work. I wonder if my clients feel this way about me?

I didn't go for a second opinion. There's no point; it hurts enough now that having a metatarsal shortened, another bone broken and carved down, and a ligament screwed to my second toe bone sounds like a pedicure to me.

I asked him what causes this to happen to a foot. He said sometimes it's hereditary. (No one I know.) Or it could from wearing heels. (Never; the closest I get are old Ariat equestrian clogs but only if it's formal.) He sees me shake my head, and adds there are other "odd causes." I bite my tongue.

This is what I know about going to a doctor: Don't mention that you train horses for a living. Or that you spend the rest of your time in the same place. He doesn't need to know you dance around with thousand-pound horses—it's how they get a bad name with doctors.

I'm still thinking of lame horses. Especially the ones that look like me; fine on the outside. I just move slower and don't warm-up out of it. People I walk with get impatient with me. I see it in their bodies more than anything they say. I try to keep up but then I get impatient with myself, as well as the pain. Is that what stoic horses do?

About then the Dude Rancher blabs about horses and the doctor mentions his concern for protecting my foot from pathogens in the barn. Like there is anything in the barn I haven't ingested for years already. There's an argument that I may have actually become a barn pathogen myself and I'm infecting the hospital. Oddly, the doctor doesn't mention thousand-pound hooves and neither do I.

Then they gave me an Easy Boot kind of brace (like those comfy velcro hoof-boots for horses) and a pair of crutches. How is it possible that I can stack hay but not be strong enough to maneuver on crutches? A new friend (we bonded over talk of lameness) is lending me her knee scooter. When I saw a man at the grocery store with one, and I limped over to him to ask questions. It traveled quick, he said, but he'd gotten bucked off it pretty hard. He says it's best for indoor use.

After surgery, I'll be on pain meds and stall rest. The Grandfather Horse spent years on stall rest and just anticipating mine is half-killing me. I notice my attempt at being stoic is giving way to being a whiner already. Spirit did better after I put a goat in his stall with him. My house is small with lots of narrow doorways and four dogs who take my care and protection extremely seriously. A goat would be more fun.

But on a high note, and humor me—I'm not singing many high notes—the Dude Rancher got me a contraption for use in the barn. It's a strap-on knee crutch; think peg-leg on a pirate. I'm sure he feels compassion for me, but it's self-preservation, too. You don't want me trapped in your house for six weeks either.

SINGLETON DREAMS: SHEDDING IN THE BEDDING

These are the dog days of summer—long and extreme. Not the kindest summer, either. My extended horse family has suffered some huge, sad losses and a few chronic health issues have flared up in my own barn. It's a bumper year for hurtful drama, flies, and humidity; something we try to avoid here in Colorado. To tell the truth, it just hasn't been a giggling, tap dancing, high-spirited season.

The thing about stress is that it doesn't matter if it's good stress—like my first book, *Stable Relation*, being published—or bad stress like doing without the pasture turnout while replacing flood-torn fences. Stress is a slow-motion weight at mid-afternoon that makes your shoes heavy and your brain thick. It's a sticky winter quilt in August, but we still need the rest.

Forget about it; it's time for the seasonal Corgi report. Enough small talk of world issues, natural disasters, and human angst. It's time to focus on shorter legs and louder voices.

Walter and Preacher Man are having a summer, too. The water in the bowl has no ice. The duck work is endless; the way they speed-waddle after flies needs to be watched constantly. And then the bunny population has exploded; there's a farm-wide illegal immigration problem that must be addressed. Job-related stress has never been higher, but the little men are Corgi Tough.

Walter is much too busy to whine about his health but his anxiety seeps out. He's anxious about meals—all four of them every day. He's anxious about feeling weaker so he's trying to act stronger, like a tiny man who needs to let the world know how crucial he is to world order. We tell him we know, but he's still working double shifts. It's an existential dilemma for Walter. He's lost confidence. That's an ailment that goats never experience. It kept Walter awake, bounding to the back door with an ear-splitting caterwaul every hour or two, night after night. Finally, I asked Walter into his crate and closed the door. We should all lay down our daily worries as easily. His snoring tells me it's possible.

Then Preacher Man, who was sleeping under the bed like a snapping turtle under a riverbank, came out and took one unlikely bound that put him on the bed. It surprised all of us. There was already a dozing Briard, Tomboy, and maybe a cat or two with all the stupid-wild danger that involves. Preacher curled up in the only space left, between my ear and the edge of the bed. That next morning, I woke up to a soft gargling moan. Safety required that he keep a sleepy eye on the door, so it was his feathery backside pushed up against my cheek. If you are going to sleep in a dogpile, these things happen.

I used to think that Preacher Man dreamed of being an only dog. That he fantasized about the two of us on a desert island with only a couch and all the raw food he could eat. That his frantic howl-oodle-ing was an attempt to clear the room for his only child fantasy. Seen that way, all the dogs could fit the same description, not to mention a couple horses, a few old cats, and one particularly eloquent donkey. Maybe they all wanted to be the singleton, the heir apparent, the one and only. I give everyone one-on-one time but was I kidding myself?

Disclaimer: I'm the human here. It's a disadvantage. I think too much. I'm alternately wracked with self-doubt or so arrogant about our herd that I march around like a prickly yucca-goddess of the high prairie. It's the dog's job to rein me in and remind me of the truth. We will always be ruled by dogs.

As this exhausting summer has worn on, my perspective has changed. I'm probably nuts; just write what I am about to say off as anthropomorphic hogwash. Recently all the barking and fending off daily farm danger seems to ring with a different message. I think I've had it backwards. What if they see me as an *only* person? *Their* only person. What if I'm the real singleton? The little Corgi men have lost a few humans in the past, as rescue dogs all know, so tag-teaming me seems the smart thing to do, in the bathroom and out in the world. To them, it's all about herding the prize. Me.

I have a big day today. I need to be alert and articulate—and I'm not sure I'm up to the task. But I slept in a dogpile of passion and persistence.

They say behind every great man is a woman. Well, I'm not a great man. I'm a tired woman and my feet hurt. But at those same feet are two yapping and frapping Corgis. I am their singleton and they have my back. Marvel at their power! Corgi energy can light a city; they can yodel a prairie opera. Die hard optimists, these corgis are not at all fearless, but they act that way. I've learned it from them. May I return tonight victorious—with liver treats and beer!

Fair warning to evil-doers and curmudgeons: I'm running on Corgi power today. The other word for that is invincible.

GOATS: A DIFFERENT TWELVE-STEP PROGRAM

It just hasn't been the same since Sumo died. He was my last old goat and a card-carrying anarchist. He'd been un-fencible here since day one. I miss coming into the barn in the morning to find the feed cabinet pried open and supplement containers flung into the runs. Goats are generous to horses that way. I miss those tell-tale turdettes sprinkled around the tack room after he executed search and seizure drills looking for any hidden illicit horse treats. I miss his witty and urbane conversation. *Blah. Blah. Bla-aa-aah.*

Having a goat is like a twelve-step program for Type-A perfectionists who have allegro-phobia. (That's a fear of being late; disorders love company.) Goats are not burdened with polite social conventions and certainly have no inclination at all to please people. It's why they're so attractive.

Then I heard about a wether goat (neutered male) in a friend-of-a-friend sort of way. A herd needed downsizing to help the owner's health condition. I made the call and was on my way. When I got there, the woman lead me to a milking herd in a pasture and explained that the wether hadn't been hand-tamed. This would have been the moment to reconsider. She said he'd probably only been caught once and that was when the vet came for the neutering or *banding*. Use your imagination; he wasn't about to surrender peacefully.

Note to self: My next get-rich-quick plan is a pay-per-view event pitting a goat kid against pairs of post-sixty-year-old women competing as a team. Or anyone else who has a clear idea of how easy it is to maintain order and calm.

It took both of us to wrestle a lead around the four-month-old kid's neck and pull him away from the herd. Now he's twice as certain that something is terribly wrong. He's caught but he frantically flings his body upside down and back toward the herd. He doesn't stop throwing his little body in all directions at once, bracing all four legs in a convulsion of hysteria. His now-previous owner goes to get me some organic goat feed to take home, and I hoist him up in my arms, as his screams double. I wonder why I don't just put my helmet on in the morning after my shower and leave it there.

By the time I settle him in back of the extended cab of my truck, he'd kicked his feed, spraying it evenly through the truck, and then tipped his water on top of it. Finally, he settles, but maybe a bit too much. Driving away, I adjust my rear-view mirror and he's staring at me with his spooky, rectangular pupils. He hates me.

Is this wether a rescue? Well, yes and no. He had pretty much the same option every other young wether has. Milking herds, faced with the prospect of feeding neutered males all winter when they will not breed or give milk in the spring... Well, you know what happens. And around this age. So, he's a different kind of rescue, I guess, not that he cares. He hates me.

We arrive home and his little jaw is still clenched so hard it looks like he's pursing his lips. His little body is stiff and braced as I carry him to his pen. He's still on the walking strike. Then he hides behind a barrel in his pen and starts a hunger strike. Goats are ruminants and a crash diet will kill him. In the morning, he still hasn't eaten and he's thin. His hay and water were left untouched; even his grain ignored. Maybe without his herd, he's dead anyway.

I dosed him with some probiotics and practically needed a

tire iron to get it on his tongue. He was disconsolate so I moved him out to a grassy place but couldn't let him loose. I knew better than to think I could catch him again. I had to tie him and he ran hard on the rope, hit the end at breakneck speed, and flipped in the air. The panic repeated several times, with so much anxiety that it was heartbreaking to watch. It got worse if I came closer.

But Edgar Rice Burro was in the adjoining turn-out. He sauntered over and pretended to eat. There was no grass on his side of the fence but he befriended this newcomer because that's his way. The little goat's jaw loosened for the first time. In a few moments, he was grazing along next to Edgar, who spent the rest of the day right there.

Hello, my name is Anna. I'm Type-A and powerless over my need to tidy. I sometimes get worried; I can think silly things are important. It blinds me to the beauty of life when I obsessively focus and compulsively worry about the dark ways of the world. In those moments, the barn elders look frail and mortal. Even a howling tenor bray from Edgar Rice Burro isn't enough to remind me to lighten up; I'm nothing special. I cannot control the universe, or even my heart. And no one elected me Boss Mare of the country anyway.

I could post a huge sign in the barn with the Serenity Prayer on it and chant it on the hour ...*God, grant me the serenity to accept the things I cannot change, etc.* ...or I could just get a goat and name him Arthur. His first trick doesn't look like much; walking up and taking some grain from my hand. It's a tiny truce. He hates me.

***

It's life and death out there every single day but you don't have to follow along like a sheep. You can bleat the goat anthem, steal some horse treats, and head-butt your way to donkey friendship. Watch me make the dogs bark.

***

I'm good with that because in the end, it's always that quality of-life question. Mine as well as his.

Oops, gotta go. The black tarp that was hanging on a fence panel is now bleating, making its way west across a pen, and scaring the bejeebers out of the horses.

WHAT ARE YOU SAVING FOR GOOD?

My parents grew up in the Great Depression. We kept things "for good." It was the first Easter after we lost our farm and we'd moved across four states and settled in a tract house, trying to pass for suburbanites. I was nine and mortally wounded from seeing my horse sold, so in a vain effort, my mother got me the only brand new dress I ever remember having. We were poor relations and my mother's aunt sent us boxes of hand-me-downs from their girls. My older sister got them first, so I could see my wardrobe coming at a distance. This Easter dress was precious, partly because it was a washed-out green color and it had a full skirt with a layer of actual chiffon on top, and partly because it was the same year that I had set my heart on becoming a nun. It was the only dress I ever loved. So, after wearing it to church once, I kept it "for good."

You know how this ends; a year later we'd moved to the edge of town, I'd already outgrown the dress, in more ways than one, and I was still whining about horses. The other thing that stuck was my mother's frugal habit; everything special was kept safely out of reach.

Many years later, my mother bought me a beautiful wooden bench with carved horse heads, and a brand-new butter-soft bridle. Well, that's an exaggeration. She had passed away but she would have wanted me to have them. Okay, probably not, but it's what I'd like to believe. Cats took to sleeping on the bench but the bridle went in a show bag where I kept it "for good," because I'm a grand-daughter of the Depression.

The dark side of frugal runs to being stingy. It's the worry that comes from fear and lack; the feeling that nothing good will happen and if something does, somehow, it must be held separate. We did it with Easter dresses, birthday bubble bath, and mother's heirloom sterling—which I saw for the first time in my life just a month before she died. And of course, she and I held back the best in ourselves as well, in a dark closet, while we struggled on. We didn't know another way.

At the same time, my other family—the one in the barn—was giving me their generational hand-me-downs, too. Good horses encouraged me to open my heart and trust that good things could happen. They rewarded me constantly. The more I let go of my fears and reached out to my horses with kindness, instead of worry and limitation, the steadier we got. Sometimes people told me that I had a push-button horse; some magical creature that you might find locked in a glass cabinet, but we knew the truth. My horse and I took what we had and polished it up a little every day. We became larger than the sum of our parts. Most of us stick with horses because we end up better people than we were when we started. That happened for me.

My poor mother was wary from loss and so, trying to control outcome, she labeled things good and bad—mostly bad. But even that was too meager; horses taught me the real challenge is choosing between love and fear.

A few years back when it was time to start my young mare, she inherited the Grandfather Horse's patched and faded first winter blanket, for good luck, and that brand-new bridle because she's good enough before she even starts.

So, that's my question; what are you holding back—keeping for good—in the barn? I know you have a saddle pad squirreled away. And maybe some nice breeches. You know the waist could get tighter on those if they hide in the drawer too long. Besides, they were on sale. Let yourself have them, for crying out loud.

And what about your horse? Do you keep a critical eye peeled because you need to prepare for the worst? Are you quick to find fault, judging your rides harshly before other riders have the chance? Do you strive for perfection so hard that your horse feels your constant doubt? Or do you never actually ask for his best work because the two of you are nothing special to start with? And then, are you conservative in rewarding him because he was never quite good enough? Finally, does he act like he's carrying the entire Great Depression on his back? Is he right?

Then fear has won and it's time for love to rise up. Remember what horses have always meant to you and feel your heart warm, as your shoulders soften. Then say thank you, just like your mother taught you. Ask for your horse's very best work, because you respect him and you both deserve it. Then become the rider you need to be to receive it. Sit tall and proud; you've already won just being there. Most of all don't let the tatters and tears of everyday life convince you that your horse is any less than perfect and ready to shine. Reward that flawless possibility because it isn't bought with money or luck, and the more you affirm it, the stronger it gets. Then with a freeing breath, know that we are all made of stardust; this perfection is inside us every day.

Sure, bad things happen and fear is a natural response. But we shouldn't let it change who we are. It's up to us to remember the stuff we are made of.

There will always be two stories about horses. One is that they are brainless tools; too crazy or lazy or just not worth the effort. That you'll always be a victim of a horse's whims and habits unless you dominate him to a stupor. The other story is that horses are mythical creatures with brave hearts who lift and carry us in perfect unity. That together, we can break free of earthly limitations.

Both stories actually start the same way. After that, we get just about what we think we deserve.

HEALTH INSURANCE
AND HORSE DREAMS

I'm due to have foot surgery on Friday. It's like preparing for a trip that I don't get to take. All the stress of canceling work, stocking up on feed and supplements, prepping the barn for winter, as well as all the indoor work, so that I can keep my post-surgery foot higher than my heart for stall rest detention. I plan on following the doctor's directions because I don't want to have this forced couch-vacation one day longer than necessary, but I'm fraught, frustrated, and fearful. All F-words, I notice.

And if horses have taught me one thing, it's that ruminating on problems only makes things worse. *(But there is going to be something wicked-sharp cutting into my skinny, bony foot!)* And aren't I the one always insipidly chirping about breath and focus? *(But...but it hurts.)* Is it too soon to breathe my way into a horse dream instead of having an anxiety runaway?

There's a particular dream that's always just on the backside of my eyelids. It's the first dream I remember having as a kid and it recurred with alarming frequency for years; one of those dreams that was so very real that each of my senses remembered it long after I woke.

Here's a surprise: In the dream, I'm on a horse. First I notice a breeze on my face; just enough to move the hair on my shoulders. It's because I'm moving. When I open my eyes the rest the way and look down, a thigh, much more muscular and tan than mime, rests on the shoulder of a bay and white pinto. It was like I was wearing another body. Do you ever have dreams where it's you but you don't recognize yourself?

Then the breeze picks up, the rhythm get smoother, and I feel the one-two-three waltz of the canter begin. And my sit-bones begin the wave motion and the rest of my spine follows, one vertebra at a time. I'm barefoot; no boot or stirrup. There's no holding on or letting go, we just cover ground. My hands play in his mane.

The land is not a place I know. There are low, gradual hills and huge open valleys with tall yellow grass and patches of random shrubs. The sun is always at our backs.

On we go, through and over and around, but the landscape doesn't alter our balance. Sometimes his hooves smash sage plants and the air filled with the rich aroma, and I felt his ribs take a deep inhale that I match.

So, that's the dream. We aren't on a journey. No one chases us. There are no weather disasters. We never get tired. There's never a lather, or even a sweat, but there's a warmth that feels like the glow of embers buried deep between us.

The dream started before I began to ride. I had already broken my little-girl-nose on a Suffolk ram named Grandpa, and I had very little sense of smell. I was shy and awkward; my pasty white bird legs were never that supple. The dream wasn't based on anything I knew in my waking life, but the ride was offered whenever I closed my eyes.

When I was nine, we packed up the station wagon and moved to Washington state. I recognized land from my dream when we drove through Montana. The dream followed me through high school, and beyond, continuing after I left home and came to Colorado. Years passed and it came less frequently.

When my Grandfather Horse was young, he got pretty tense on one of our early trail rides. While my friend waited, I trotted him in a circle to help him relax. We eased into a canter and let the circle get slowly larger. My friend and I had joked about never raising our eyes above our horse's ears because it was wild-flower season and the ground was as ornate as a Persian carpet.

As Spirit and I cantered on, we crossed a patch of frosty-green sage and his hooves made a slightly different sound as they crushed it, and the herbal aroma from the dream seasoned the real Colorado prairie. My legs felt his inhale as deep as my own. Every second was hours long and my senses expanded. I don't know if I've ever been more sensually aware of a physical moment.

Eventually my horse and I dropped down to a walk and we rejoined my friend, who said we'd both looked a little odd. The dream never came again at night, but it somehow transmuted to my conscious world. The dream travels with me now, as real as a horse's heart. Has your horse given you peace of mind?

It's before dawn. Surgery is scheduled for about three hours from now. I admit it; I'm really afraid. Then at the last minute, we found out there's some huge insurance snafu; a problem that we couldn't resolve on the phone after closing hours. I don't know if the surgery is a go or not, and I'm still fraught, frustrated, and fearful.

At the same time, horses are a parable for everything we know in life. A few circles, some deep breathing, and we'll get on with the ride.

HOW THE BARN BECAME A CHURCH

Were you born in a barn? Not me, but I wish. I lived in the tiny asphalt-shingle house just south of the barn.

The barn was huge and white, with doors that rolled open wide enough that even the big tractor passed through with room to spare. There were two tall silos on the east side, and a loft with arched rafters that formed a dome high above the hay. You could climb the ladder up to the loft and build forts with the barn cats. The light that came in through small windows, diffused by dust and hay, had a way of making things look sacred, like those holy cards with prayerful saints in halos. Our barn was simply the warmest, most inviting place in the world. And much bigger than a church. What was I supposed to think?

Is this not the barn story you expected this time of year?

It isn't everyone's favorite holiday. Some of us have been hiding in the barn to avoid it for years. For some of us, a Hallmark commercial is enough to trigger dark memories. Not everyone is up to the effort of marketing the image of an ideal family. Some of us don't even have human family. Or we might be mourning loss or just in need of a quiet place for introverts. And sometimes a barn is more welcoming to black sheep. It's less about defending spiritual beliefs and more about finding a safe haven.

It's that time for my annual PSA about holiday visits to the barn. You can leave the bells at home. Enough with the antler head-bands and chipper seasonal music. This barn is their home and it's rude of us to bring our tinsel and lights and white-hot stress along. We are such agitators, waving carrots in the air and calling in high-pitched voices, as if announcing our arrival makes the party complete.

Hush. This barn is sacred. We are guests here. Speak the native language and try to blend in with the herd; lick and chew. Are you ever humbled with respect for these incredible creatures? Is the sound of them eating any less holy than a Gregorian chant?

"We are all creatures of one family." —St. Francis of Assisi

It's okay if you got yourself a horse blanket or a new saddle pad. Maybe you brought yourself peppermint treats to give out. It's fine; we humans get nervous if it's too quiet. But your horse doesn't dream of those things. He dreams of safety and peace. The equine translation of that is *release.*

No matter how many times we hear that horses want a smaller cue, that less is more, and that the best reward is release, we fight it. We want to give more, have more, do more. We fund studies about whether horses prefer patting or scratching, when a still hand is utterly eloquent. We still can't believe that release—not asking for anything—can be a reward. It's almost anti-human. Like they would be better off without us.

So, some of us train our horses to be needy, to fill that lack within us, as if insecurity was intelligence and fear was normal.

And some of us try it their way. We listen to their calming signals. When they avert their eyes and look away, they're telling us that we can be less aggressive; that they mean us no harm. Listen to them. Take the cue, breathe slower, and turn your body noise down. Then wait. Ask for nothing. Give nothing. Be still and breathe with empty hands. You are enough just as you are.

What if the herd had it right all along? What if when we lay down our perceived wants and needs, our wishing and trying, we can share that *Peace in Want of Nothing.* Release; can we give it to ourselves?

Because in the end, all the chatter about churches or barns, inns or stables, doesn't make a lick of difference. The message has always been *Peace.*

WHEN NOTHING LESS THAN HAVARTI WILL DO

I've been getting the stink eye from Preacher Man.

It happens. He's a member of the Long and Low Club, and while charging through the yard, herding the indifferent ducks from outside their fence, he's bound to kick up some debris. It's important work; he's moved around some in his life and he needs to get it right this time.

I'm used to big dogs that don't scuffle leaves into their own eyes but Preacher is a measly eighteen and a half pounds. He's shorter than a cat but he tries to make up for it in volume. The audible kind: If he's breathing, he's barking. So, this yodeling-si-ren-tornado of a dog had a squinty eye and I used my amateur vet/all-star wrestling skills to flush it out. By the next morning, his eye had swollen nearly closed.

***

Injured in the line of duty. They're a dangerous gang of ducks.

***

I called my vet and told them I needed to bring a dog in. "Oh, it is Walter?" She sounded hopeful. They love Walter at the front desk. I break the news that it's Preacher, but they still get us in.

I must secure Preacher Man when we drive. If I don't, my truck cab looks like the Saturday Night Live "bass-o-matic" skit, but even that doesn't inhibit his hysteric tenor, on high alert.

Sometimes when there's a pair of something—Corgis, sisters, whatever—they define each other. Meaning there's the good one, and well, the *other* one. Preacher Man is the *other*. It's what he and I have in common. Both dogs are rescues, but when the good Corgi, Walter, goes to the vet, he makes his ears wide in an affable way, tilts his head slightly away, and gives a coquettish smile. The front desk staff coos and shovels treats to him. It's one of the benefits of having a terminal diagnosis; you can do no wrong.

When we arrived at the vet an hour later, no treats were offered. Preacher wore his orange truss and two leashes, a necessity for this *other* dog. I wore the only matched pair of shoes that fit my post-surgery foot—fruity purple crocs. We're a team; I think these were my junior high school colors.

Then someone came in the waiting area with a German shepherd—off leash. How is it that people confuse the waiting area for a dog park? Or is the owner trying to impress all of us with his training skills? Nope. The shepherd takes several steps away from his owner toward us.

***

Get back. I'm scared. I mean scary.

***

As Preacher trumpets the warning, I pick him up so fast that I nearly lob him into the ceiling. On the high side, the sudden change of air pressure did disorient his bark for a moment.

Safely in an exam room, the vet stains the squinty eye to get a better look and I can see the splinter in the center of his cornea from across the table. She says removing it might cause problems. Every picture I conjure in my head is too grisly to recount. Apparently, my vet is imagining the same because she sends us to a specialist. My first canine ophthalmologist, which is actually saying something at my level of veterinary experience. On our exit, Preacher Man was offered a treat, but I couldn't warn them quickly enough so he nipped, literally biting the hand that feeds...oh, rats. He's so incredulous that a stranger would give him a treat, that he can't contain himself. Even though we work on slow treats every day. For almost two years now.

We howl and yip our way across town to the eye vet, who's double booked already, but will squeeze us in. Any ounce of optimism I had is gone and I'm wondering if there's enough money on my charge card and if Preacher will need to wear a tiny pirate eye patch.

We're settled into this second waiting room with a couple of older sleepy-eyed dogs, just as a spaniel and his human exit to the front desk to pay their bill. The human makes a show of giving her dog a treat, separated into four parts, with a very obedient sit for each crumb. The other dogs in the waiting room are all coming apart, looking for their treat, and the spaniel's human gets to think no other dog is as well-behaved as hers. By now I'd like to bark at her myself.

Finally, we go back and the vet hurries in, saying it's the first time he's ever met a dog by this name. He startles Preacher, who's barking too loud for me to tell the vet he doesn't bite. I answer a few questions during the exam, like does Preacher go outside. "He lives on a farm." The vet sighs and says well, you'll need to keep him inside then. I just let my jaw rest where it fell. The vet tech prepares to hold Preacher Man and I'm given my orders to scratch his butt on cue. The vet pulls on a visor, picks a pair of very pointy tweezers, and tells Preacher to say two Hail Mary's. And in he went.

~No veterinarians or vet techs were harmed in this procedure~

The receipt says "The foreign body was successfully removed in toto using a foreign body spud." We get two bottles of eye-drops, each given morning and night. That adds up to four doses a day. Really? I'm good but who are we kidding?

So, when we got home I explained to Preacher, eye drops in one hand and cheese in the other, that eye drops are good, just like cheese. He stands up on my knee, perfectly still, presents me his squinty eye for a drop.

***

I'll try. For you. Be careful.

***

It's an act of faith with no wrestling moves required and he blinks hard when the drop hits. He's nearly imploding, trying so hard to be good, that I get something in my eye, too. I decide to upgrade from cheap Swiss cheese to Havarti. It's wildly more than he could possibly hope for. He nips my fingers, but just a tiny bit because he really is trying to be good.

For all of us who've been bounced around some, been disappointments to our family, or reluctantly lost friends because we are *other*; because we awkwardly try too hard, or are *differently likable*—take heart and caterwaul like no one has ears. There's a full moon on the prairie tonight and a home somewhere for all of us. Let it be.

THE GRANDFATHER HORSE: WHEN ANIMALS HAVE PETS...

I have a bone to pick with my Grandfather Horse. He stole my goat.

It's hard to complain. Spirit's been my soulmate for the last twenty-nine years and I'm prone to writing sticky, sentimental stories about him. Sure, back in the day we got a little contrary with each other from time to time. And yes, he always did prefer people who didn't know how to ride. Can't fault him for that.

My Grandfather Horse's habit of keeping pets wasn't obvious at first. During the first years I boarded him there, was no real opportunity for exotic pets, so he settled for what he could find—cats mostly. I thought it was normal.

At our last boarding barn, he befriended a tiny black kitten, way too young to be on his own. Spirit threw him some grain, and when the kitten was still there the next day, getting kitten chow seemed smart, along with a little bowl for under the hay feeder. The kitten swung on Spirit's tail and climbed all over his back. He batted at my curry and left fierce claw marks on Spirit's saddle. Horses are social animals and I didn't think much about it until the kitten stepped off a gate and onto my other horse's back. Dodger came apart like the Fourth of July. The kitten didn't have any luck riding other horses in the barn either. I started to get suspicious of my Grandfather Horse.

The first year here on the farm a llama cria was born. Spirit let me know that the mom was in labor and then we both sat back to wait. Well, I sat back, while he put his head through the fence panel and stared. Two hours later, little baby Belle Starr finally wobbled away from her mom and over to touch noses with Spirit, still waiting patiently. I managed to keep them apart for almost two weeks. Perhaps you've met Belle? She's the llama who comes up to strange horses at a dead run for a nose rub. The Grandfather Horse taught her that.

The next year, a friend and I rescued a small herd of neglected donkeys. When they arrived here, the last one out of the trailer was especially fearful, teetering on hooves that looked like elf shoes. Still, he marched right up to Spirit, whose nose was through the fence panel again, and it was all over but the tattoos. We re-homed the others, but it took me weeks to settle this little donkey. If I looked out the window in the middle of the night, the Grandfather Horse and his new donkey friend would be doing the tango in the moonlight and biting each other's elbows. I never had a chance. Years later when Edgar Rice Burro arrived, it was like they were old army buddies.

You would have thought that a pair of elderly, free-range ducks would be beneath the Grandfather Horse... but they waddled back from the pond in the afternoon just in time for Spirit to toss some grain down to them. He was just showing off by that point.

It's no surprise that the horses all love him best. The mares are all besotted and the geldings act like he's Steve McQueen-cool. Even now, when half the herd doesn't know who Steve McQueen was. Sure, he does me a favor every day; he runs the young Mare-Who-Would-Be-Alpha off her hay. It probably isn't in deference to me; he does it for sport more likely. If he's having a particularly stiff day, he does it with his eyeballs. Then he gets his *faux-humble* look as Edgar Rice Burro dips his long ears with respect. Egads.

But I had plans for Arthur, the goat. It would be different this time. Really.

Arthur used to live in the next county, when he totally lucked out. He won a one-way trip in the cab of my truck. As one-way goat trips go, Arthur was wildly lucky, not that he was grateful. Goats aren't burdened with the social constrictions of gravity or good manners. He left proof of that in my truck, but you know, a good ranch truck doesn't worry about polite society either.

Arthur got a comfy pen in my smaller barn, far from Spirit but next to Edgar Rice Burro and a very amiable chestnut gelding. He was terrified, having never been around people, but I have a way with goats—and a can of grain—so I set about winning him over. I was relentless, but by the time he was tentatively taking one tiny bit of grain from my hand, he was able to break out of his pen five or six times a day. Each time Arthur got loose he bolted through the other horse runs and screeched to a stop under Spirit's belly. Resistance was futile. Eventually, I gave up bringing him back; he's been in that shady spot ever since. Now Arthur comes to gobble a handful of grain from me, but then he's gone, recklessly bounding back through the fence in an important hurry. He has priorities.

My Grandfather Horse had a mild colic this week, as the first snow storm of the season threatened. Arthur and I stayed close. Mild is a word we can only associate with colic in hindsight. All colic is serious in the beginning and my old horse is frail. He's okay now and it's still good to be king. He's the one who taught me the most important thing I know about training horses—it's all about negotiation. You see, I used to be a bit of a goat myself in my youth. I pretend to know better now.

But there they are; the Grandfather Horse is lying in the sun, napping on end of his nose, and there's Arthur. Sometimes he curls up and sleeps on top and sometimes he stands tall, marching around on that old arthritic back. Is this some sort of massage? Arthur must weigh at least sixty pounds by now and he has pointy hooves. He tries to stay on when Spirit stands up, like that kitten did, but Arthur's off in a twitch.

I'm still upset that he stole my goat, but no one can stay mad at the Grandfather Horse for long... or maybe I'm jealous of Arthur. That place on his back used to be my spot.

DOGS AND THE THINGS WE CANNOT CHANGE

Are you the kind of person who gets nervous in a new place if there isn't a dog to talk to? Do you find it easy to look through the dog spit dried on the passenger window when making a right turn in your truck? Do you have a drawer with a bunch of old dog collars with worn tags that you just can't bring yourself to throw out?

A couple of weeks ago I was at a book event standing behind a table. The author next to me said something that I didn't catch. It might have been clever. She laughed and laughed, pointing at some short white and yellow hairs on my tablecloth. Of course, there were hairs there; they matched the ones on my clothes. I still don't get the joke but it had to do with her not having a dog. I don't understand that either.

So, I didn't tell her that in my writing studio I have four dog beds and a can of compressed air to blow those same hairs out of my keyboard. It's worse; I lay proud claim to especially liking bad dogs.

Both Walter and Preacher flunked out of adoptive homes in the past because they barked too much. But it isn't like they bark all the time. Just if there is another person around. Or other dogs. Or horses. And of course, cats, but that's expected. And the llamas; they look like alien cats, after all. Besides, it's their job to ward off intruders. Okay, the truth is they'd probably both be considered reactive dogs. It's a lifestyle choice that limits their welcome; not everyone appreciates their brand of compulsive yodeling as much as me. I suppose there are those who would hold their shedding against them, too.

The pack also includes an elderly Briard, Tomboy, and Finny, a kind soul of a lab mix. We were all coasting along, dysfunctional and happy about it. Sure, Walter had that terminal diagnosis but he'd been cheerfully howling on, ignoring dozens of blood tests that said he was in a danger zone and past his expiration date. It all became our normal.

Sometimes change hits you like a sledgehammer, but for us it was more of a slow leak, almost unnoticeable above the usual yelping pitch of our lives. Gradually there was more fighting at the back door. The dogs all ate separately, but mealtime became increasingly frantic anyway. The dogs who didn't usually bark took up the habit.

It's been over two years since Walter was first diagnosed and we were told he had six months at best. If he wasn't so thin, you'd never know he was sick at all. Until lately, that is. His strength sometimes falters; he still barks too much, but with less enthusiasm. My vet told me what symptoms to look for: weight loss, vomiting, lethargy, diarrhea, no appetite. So, I watch for a physical sign.

I read somewhere that when dogs begin to weaken with age, some will want to act tough as a sort of self-defense. Maybe it's like that but Walter has gotten quite aggressive with a deep and constant growl, even toward me. His hackles are always visible, like he must threaten us to prove his strength. His muscles quiver most of the time.

We all feel his stress. Walter attacks Tomboy most often and she guards against it, growling and barking back. Preacher joins in but always afraid of getting stepped on, he nips from behind while barking hysterically. Timid Finny worries, waits for a quiet moment, and then pounces on Walter when he least expects it. Breaking up fights is a constant, while all the time thinking this isn't who we are. It's not what we do.

Yes, we've tried every herbal available and taken all reasonable advice. Walter lives in a Thundershirt now (a coat that helps dogs with anxiety). I can't tell if it calms him but it hides some bald patches. He hates being separated and hates being with us. He constantly paces. I've talked to the vet about anxiety medication but as compromised as his liver is, she says it would be a dangerous idea. Now I think maybe the rest of us could use some medication.

I continue to look for a sign. Even as I continue to ignore all the signs.

Last weekend, I took Walter to Denver for some TTouch and a massage. I worried that he might have a second condition—a sore back maybe. Watching him get his treatment gave me a chance to see him with different eyes. In the beginning, he was restless, he winced a couple of times, and eventually relaxed deeply. Seeing his body finally soft reminded me what he was like before all this started.

So, our pack is a mess lately. We all have some pretty spectacular short comings; we get things wrong in this slow-motion war, myself included. Care-giving is exhausting, but Walter is one of us, even on a bad day. We'll see him through and try to remember that it isn't really us that he's fighting.

Rescue dogs are all the rage. It's a quality of life transaction; we want to give them a better life and we get the same in return. The plan is always to have more good days than bad, but sometimes that isn't possible. Then we lower our expectations and say thank you. We're just hoping for a few more moments of that sweet late-afternoon sun.

ON BRAVERY AND BEING AN OLD GRAY MARE

Do you have a mentor? Someone you respect who's just a few strides ahead of you, and when they go through the door, they give it a shove so there's a gap left for you? Or are you on your own personal *road less traveled?* Are you just where you thought you'd be at this age, or has life taken a few unplanned turns? It isn't good or bad, so much as bewildering. Because as you look ahead, you can't see anyone loitering around, dispensing wisdom and encouragement. It might even look like the *road never traveled at all.*

I was asked to write something on strong women. The suggested title was *One Tough Mother,* with a double meaning: The literal one is somebody who loves hard and does the work required to bring others up in this world. And the other one is slang that's used to describe challenging work or even life itself. I can't tell if it's an insult or a back-handed compliment.

Courage and strength, or the lack of it, has come up in a few conversations lately, usually related to a huge change in life or the process of recovering from an illness or injury. For my part, I'm still limping about in a post-surgery boot, teetering on that thin line between acting optimistic, but still being time-frustrated and feeling a bit sorry for myself, so I was all ears.

They all had different details, but in each story things hadn't been quite right and looking back there were signs. Eventually things came apart, the truth was uncovered, and lives got threatened because it takes something that big to get our attention. The stories are painful and awkward but there was some dark humor, too. One friend who survived serious surgery lamented that the drug that would lessen the chance of recurrence, also seemed to have the side effect of making her husband seem especially annoying. Should they have a warning label for that?

And most of us judge ourselves harshly on a good day, but we add a special dollop of sad guilt when we aren't at our best. Even as we recite all the proper, mundane platitudes and hunker down to wait for the worst. It's all we can do and it never feels like enough.

And as I listen to my friends, I am always aware of how much courage is revealed in conversations about weakness. It isn't false modesty, it's because ideals like bravery get lost in the fog of proceeding. We're too busy doing what it will take for the next step—how to survive, what to adapt, how to resolve it. We're like work horses; we keep our heads low, lean into the harness, and pull. When that doesn't work, we may shed some tears or rant some creative profanities or give in for that day. But then we slide back into the harness and pull some more. Progress is slow and the finish line isn't always visible.

That might be because the view is behind us. Bravery and perseverance are best seen in hindsight. If you ask most of us, we say we've never done anything special. We just took things one day at a time, even when we hated it. We just did the thing that needed doing that day. When we hear a story of someone else overcoming an obstacle, we see their courage and cheer them on, but are blind to our own. We're even strong in our humility. (Okay, not every minute, but still…)

If I could change one thing about women of a certain age, I wish we'd stop apologizing for our age.

I wish we'd brag more about our scars and our scares—and take credit for surviving. How did we ever get so impressed with youth? In our capitalistic culture, we've passed our expiration date for being a demographic; retailers ignore us because we don't buy cheap, shiny things, instead preferring a sunset with the company of an old dog. We're comfortable in boots that are as well broken in as we are. Do you realize the power we hold?

We are like elder horses. They're prey and they know it, but they still maintain a place of strength, while being sensitive and vulnerable. Sure, elder horses get more respect from their herd than we do, but then we could do a better job of claiming our victories with their confidence and grace.

I'm at an awkward age. Life is changing and I don't know what's coming. I'd love to have a mentor up ahead, but I might do better to look behind me and then shake a fist and howl at the path. Because maybe the reason we can't see a mentor up ahead is that we have become that sage entity. It might have happened when we were busy *not* taking any credit for all that we've become since we were silly girls.

There is an old song that has run on a loop forever; it's the first horse song I learned as a kid. "*The old gray mare, she ain't what she used to be, many long years ago.*" I thought it was a sad song with a chirpy beat but I finally looked it up. One version says it's about Lady Suffolk, the first horse recorded as trotting a mile in less than two and a half minutes, back in 1843. The small print reads that she was over ten years old.

Nope. The old gray mare ain't what she used to be. She's better—even faster and stronger where it matters. Let's sprint the rest of the way. Even with a limp, it's beautiful to see our kind of innate courage and strength of experience; the kind that has moved mountains in the past and isn't afraid to do it again.

I don't generally take much pride in being a human, but this week I've had pause to stand taller and be grateful. I just love us. We should take a moment to congratulate our-ripe-selves for becoming who we are. And if I see you on the street and call you an old gray mare, it's because it's the strongest compliment I know.

VALENTINE'S DAY AND A GOAT TAIL -I MEAN TALE

Is it too soon to say the word? Sure, there's more snow coming. You'd be nuts to pack away the tank heaters and long johns. Still, there's a change in the light and the calendar agrees. The coldest part of winter is past and for some of us, Valentine's Day is a cross between New Year's and the first day of spring. Horse people have their own sense of time. Let's toast with hot chocolate.

We made it! If you have an elder in your herd, breathe a secret sigh. He's managed to steal another base and the game plays on. Each winter has a new set of challenges and it isn't like the old ones have been resolved. The Grandfather Horse is still arthritic and his unsightly lump hasn't gone away.

Of course, he had his annual gastric emergency. I was recuperating from foot surgery and on a knee scooter when it happened. I called the vet and sat down on the scooter, resting my cast on the fence panel, while I watched him shift weight and furrow his brow. Then he walked down the run, sniffed my hair, and carefully laid down almost touching me. I checked the time and the pain in his eyes. Was this the day?

The Grandfather Horse is coming thirty. It's an old thirty. If you can look past the elephant in the room, it's almost laughable. We reminisced about close calls while we waited for the vet. Like that time two years ago, in the midnight ground blizzard, when he couldn't stand up. And he never lets me forget the famous near-death emergency sheath cleaning incident. Okay, it *was* pretty funny.

Eventually the vet arrived to find the two of us sprawled the width of the run. He probably wonders if today is the day, too. Nope. Not today.

Less than a month later the Grandfather Horse started spitting out *all* his chewed-up hay. He'd been spitting out a random wad here and there for years, sometimes keeping a chaw in his cheek, but this morning, it's two entire flakes of hay chewed-up and spit out in a mushy pile.

It's not that I'm cynical. Not exactly, but at lunch time I place one perfect flake of the greenest, leafiest alfalfa in his feeder. Consider it a reality check. The Grandfather Horse has grown persnickety about the exact texture of hay that he likes over the last decade, but he did it again. Spitting out alfalfa is like spitting out chocolate cake. I made the call.

The vet found a loose tooth and dang, it was on his good side. It's been four winters ago now that he had that nasty infection on the opposite side, resulting in a complicated extraction and a long recuperation. I swore I wouldn't put him through something like that again. The vet assures me it's so loose, he can almost get it with his fingers. I agree, but then he can't get a good hold on the tooth. Anesthesia is tricky with an old horse, but there's a quick shot, and the tooth is out in a blink. Then it's a full hour of trying to keep him balanced until he can stand on his own. This is the scary part; all four of us humans try to act casual but no one takes an eye away for an instant. Once again, today isn't the day.

I'd love to say the Grandfather Horse is as good as new, but that isn't the way it works. At this age, they never come back all the way. It's a negotiation and he still spits out most of his hay.

I hesitate to write about my Grandfather Horse at this point. People always tell me they cry and that isn't my goal. I swear, this is a happy story. Please don't feel sorry for his old heart…

Last week he cantered a few strides in the snow and stayed on his feet. And the sun is getting warmer for his midday naps. Sometimes I see the two mares he gets turned out with cantering in circles, while he stands in the middle, lunging them with his eyeballs. It's good to be king.

I suppose I should report one more injury. Arthur the goat, who loves to race the horses to turnout, bounded past me like that old riddle; what's black and white and red all over? The blood splatter was so vibrant and far-flung that it startled me—especially on the run like that. Goat tying isn't my event, so I went back the barn table and shook the grain can. Arthur bounded back just as quickly, blood cheerfully flying in all directions. It was the very end of his tail and it was missing. The very last vertebra of his tail was exposed—sticking out like just one finger at the end of a sleeve. The blood was starting to clot, so I dumped some grain out and ran for the amateur vet's best friend: Google. I was careful choosing my search words, but no need. Dozens of articles appeared instantly. Apparently, it isn't a rare thing with goats and they recover without much help. I managed to clean it up some, but as previously stated, goat tying isn't my thing.

Earlier, as I was mucking chewed-up hay out of the Grandfather Horse's run, I'd found a small patch of white hair still attached to a hunk of skin. It was bordering the next run, but that occupant is a bay. I thought it was odd, but then mice and snakes get baled up with the hay all the time. Egads, that must have been Arthur's tail scalp.

If there were witnesses, no one was speaking up. In U.S. criminal law, guilt is proven by *means*, *motive*, and *opportunity*. Those pointy little hooves might be *motive* enough; Arthur does pace around on the Grandfather Horse's back at nap time. *Opportunity* is a no-brainer; Arthur is always as close as kin. As for *means*—well, those long old front teeth are about the only ones the Grandfather Horse has left.

The evidence was all circumstantial. Besides, we don't have

a democracy here. Like I said, don't feel sorry for his old heart. Game on. It's still good to be the king.

A BETTER NAME FOR CHRONIC LAMENESS

It was the first day that the notion of chronic lameness got personal. My Grandfather Horse was young but he'd severely damaged a tendon in his front leg. My vet explained to me that he would most likely need two years of stall rest. *Two years*. We recovered, not perfectly, but good enough for another twelve years of happy riding before the injury recurred. This time it didn't heal well, and during the stall rest/detention, arthritis overtook his back. Chronic. Retired.

Horse owners aren't surprised. For all their thundering gallops and powerful beauty, it ends up that horses are quite frail. Lots of us have horses standing in our pastures to prove it. Chronic lameness is like a kind of purgatory; it doesn't go away and it isn't quite fatal.

Then about five years ago, I developed chronic lameness myself. In my case, it came on slowly. I got some orthotics, compartmentalized the pain, and my compassion for my herd members with chronic lameness evolved. You could call it a weird reverse anthropomorphism: I didn't see them in my image, so much as myself in theirs. I tried to mimic their stoic calm but as my foot degenerated, just gritting my teeth got more difficult. Purgatory.

Then I got lucky; I gave in to the pain. I had surgery that repaired my foot: some cutting and sawing, five screws, a lever to replace a joint, and a fencing staple to hold my big toe together. Seems like the podiatrist's version of a barn repair using twine and duct tape perhaps? That was four months ago. My foot has less pain and I'm grateful. But I lost strength, my foot is still much larger than the other, and just like too many horse injuries, it's better than it was but nowhere near brand new. But this is real life, after all, and I'm aware that others have it much worse. So, by comparison, I'll call it luck.

Around this time, a rescue horse arrived at my barn; a mid-life mare with kind eyes in need of help. The details of her situation weren't unusual. She was neglected; the owner was not remotely repentant. He wound up with a tax write-off for "donating" her to rescue but more to the point, she was safe. I thought she was just laying over at my barn for a night, waiting for a ride to the rescue. But over the course of the next week, there were two non-conflicting vet reports and negotiations between two rescues; people had opinions, misunderstandings, and the best intentions. In the end, we all got pushed toward the answer no one wanted. Somehow, in our crazy world, this passed as luck for this mare, too. Rescue isn't for sissies, but that isn't what this story is about. *To say that all my best teachers have been horses is a draft-horse-sized understatement.*

I bedded her down in a pen with the good company of a kind donkey and a respectful mini horse. She was grateful, but even that was too much. The donkey was excused from the pen and she ate well and drank more water than she'd even seen in months. The mare was still very reluctant to move, either in her pen or during the vet checks, but at the same time, no real limp. One of her shoulders had an old injury, severe enough to get retirement in a pasture, like we do. Then over time spent shifting her weight to ease the pain of her damaged shoulder, the other leg failed. Her knee, opposite the bad shoulder, blew up large and somewhere in the process, her hocks were damaged as well. And that's why she had no real limp. By definition, a limp requires one good leg and she didn't have that. Watching her over the next days, I came to understand the strength of will she exerted just to stay on her feet.

But the weather was kind and I kept her hay close. Concerned for her pain, the vet prescribed Bute twice a day. The mare resisted the syringe but I was patient. Over the next few days of repeated dosing, it had no discernible effect on her pain. I curried her each day, trying to soften her tight neck muscles. She clearly wasn't comfortable with the attention, so I went even slower and thought of her life out on the prairie. Horses run for joy, I think, but more important, it's their defense and escape. There must have been coyotes stalking her. She had to know that she was almost helpless. Did she bluff her way past them, like some smart cats will, to face down a dog rather than start a chase?

When you work with rescue horses, it's smart to have some discipline. So, I cared for her but I kept a rein on my emotions. At one point, I lamented to a woman with one of the rescues that she was about the kindest mare I'd met. "Never met one in this situation that wasn't," was her response. So, I fed and curried, and above all, respected her for a few days. Her body didn't change. The pain was constant but her eyes got a little softer.

On the last day, I offered reiki to her, and anything else I could think of. I tried to explain. She came close to eating an entire bale of sweet alfalfa. The vet arrived in the afternoon and the final decision was made. When the time came, I asked the extra people to leave and then fed my horses to distract them. We walked the mare out of their view, but not far enough to stress her needlessly. I kept my breathing long and deep as I held the lead for the vet, who was kind and compassionate in her task. The mare died as she lived; she held her ground fiercely, fighting to stand, until she was free.

I'm not sharing this story because she was an exceptional mare—she wasn't. This is just what an ordinary horse, pushed to the extreme, does. But in the instant she passed, my complacent understanding of what chronic lameness meant to a horse deepened from my tiny human experience of it. Her legacy of stoic courage taught me a better name for this painful mess: Chronic Toughness.

TRAINING THE THINGS WE TAKE FOR GRANTED

Lethargy. Preacher Man flattens himself to the marginally cool linoleum floor with his legs splayed behind him. Sweltering with a non-specific stickiness. Flies. More flies. Dilly-dallying. These are the wilting Dog Days of Summer, named for Sirius, the Dog Star. No connection to the napping habits of dogs so deflated by the heat that a sploot position looks inviting.

Preacher Man is having a good summer. I haven't been able to find the toenail clippers and sometimes a good day can be best described by what doesn't happen. And yes, he still barks too much. Or it might be a previously un-diagnosed case of canine Tourette's. It's a syndrome fairly common among horse-women as well.

In my experience, rescue dogs fall into two categories. Some are pragmatic; they stand in the front door and take a long look from the couch to the kitchen, assessing the possibilities. Immediately satisfied with the accommodations, they circle three times and fall asleep hugging the cat. Everyone resumes a peaceful routine with just a bit more dog hair in it. Everyone gets to feel magnanimous.

The other category is like entering long-term addiction therapy with your new stalker. Sure, herding dogs are a bit of a challenge on the rescue spectrum.

***

No! I'm innocent. This incarceration is a big mistake.

***

The jailers at the rescue shrugged; all the dogs desperately plead their innocence. Jailers agreed.

As for me, I began to train the things we take for granted. The everyday habits that define normal. My first task was convincing Preacher that the cats were not agents of the devil. I know what you're thinking; it's pretty much true that they are, but we're not a species-racist farm. We do not tolerate intolerance. We have a goat to prove it.

On day one, there's the big tabby cat sitting nonchalantly in the doorway to my studio and Preacher warned me like an air raid siren all day. Every hour-and-a-half or so, he paused to catch his breath and I gave him a cookie. It's positive reinforcement for the split second of quiet but positive training also requires a split second of hindsight… that instant of connecting the dots. But Preacher knows if he slows down even that much, his past might catch up. Instead he thinks that I have given him the cookie to keep his strength up in battle, and the one-sided fight begins again. Eventually Preacher wins when the cat gets bored enough to leave. Preacher settles under my chair, satisfied.

***

I'm sure trying too hard is just the ticket; I'll prove I'm indefensible. Or indispensable. One of those words.

***

How am I doing at training Preacher to be normal? First, I decided to take the high moral ground and pretend he was never housebroken in the first place. I did it for my own sanity. And his.

The hardest training had to be done after dark when the monsters roam. I guess I thought all Corgis slept belly up and snored like your weird uncle. Preacher spent the first year sleeping under the bed. The second year, he came out and tentatively pressed his backside into my ear, keeping one eye open, ready to launch across the room in attack mode should a mass-murderer or a stray cat wander by in the dark. After an hour or two, he went back under the bed. It was just too much responsibility, even for him.

But lately Preach manages to sleep through a couple of nights a week. He still must face the door, but sometimes the back of his little flat head presses hard against my cheek. Sometimes in the dark, his nose rises up and falls back toward me. All the way back, like a contortionist, till his white throat glows all the way to his belly. I exhale long and he flips around on the bed like a sturgeon out of water. We forget where we came from for a little while and our inner puppies fall into a fearless sleep.

Normal is like gravity; a steady force for balance.

Come morning, Preacher Man is back on task, ferocious that the Dude Rancher has the audacity to use the bathroom. I remember to let him outside before I sweep. Preacher seems to know an alternate use for broomsticks and he's trained me a new normal on that.

Sometimes I think I understand Preacher Man just a little too well. It's easy to find danger at every turn. To feel that the world is a scary place and any connection we have found will fray and break. Sometimes amid the stress of fearing for the worst, we let our habits change and before we know it, a purr sounds like growl. It's hard to imagine that in a still quiet moment, you could just trust yourself. That in a moment of vulnerability, you could choose to feel safe.

What they don't tell you about rescue is that it's an inside job.

A CAUTIONARY TALE ABOUT SLEEPING AROUND

We heard about Arthur, who had reached that certain age in the life of a young goat, just as we were mourning the loss of our old goat. It was kismet. Against the odds, Arthur managed to have a future after all, not that he was grateful. I was just starting to wear the little bleater down when the Grandfather Horse stole him from me. I'm cranky about it because goats are an antidote for a Type-A personality with a time obsession. Not that I have those issues. As long as there's a goat in the barn.

It's all Fun and Games...

Right away Arthur started sleeping around. He showed no concern for my feelings at all. Sure, he still came to me for a handful of grain now and then, but I had to coax him way too long. I don't mean to sound petty but he didn't seem to understand that I had saved him from being someone's soup.

Every day he'd wantonly throw himself on the ground, reclining with an ear carelessly tossed over his shoulder in the shadow underneath the Grandfather Horse. Or nap spine to spine with someone, anyone, randomly moving through the herd. He was carefree, seductively sprawling without a concern for decorum. Egads. I don't care about decorum either, but it irked me. Sometimes he was too busy head-butting Bhim, the mini, to even take grain from my hand at all. It was embarrassing. Then a month ago, he discovered my fingers were capable of scratching that itchy place on nub of his head. It was a miracle; he had no idea I had any real talent. It was a huge step, but still, he made me beg to do it.

…until someone gets hurt.

Then it happened. I came out for some evening air and Arthur was lying half-way under the Grandfather Horse. Obviously, that wasn't unusual. I went to give the Grandfather Horse a scratch, and that's when I noticed a fully-weighted hoof on one of Arthur's back legs. It had been there a while; Arthur wasn't struggling. It took an effort to release him because old horses get planted sometimes. Arthur was quivering and there was an unnatural twist to that leg. The skin wasn't broken, but the leg felt all wrong. Not to mention that it was all wrong that Arthur even let me touch it.

I grabbed a rope and pulled my Grandfather Horse out of the run, so Arthur would be safe. Naturally, Arthur struggled to his feet and limped after his horse. The injured leg never touched the ground; I could see the feather hairs on that leg quivering with pain. We went into the north pen, away from other horses at least. Arthur hobbled to the manure pile—it's his favorite place. And I started making the calls.

This is my biggest fear; I hate this part. I've got an animal in pain and I'm calling in all directions. My equine vet has helped with my goats in the past, and the after-hours answering service told me that he was the vet on call…great news. But they won't take a message, insisting he's an equine vet. I let her know we have a goat history, but she is firm. And it's too late to un-say "goat" so I hang up. I call another emergency vet but they refer me to yet another number to call. I leave a message for that vet and follow the directions to text them 911 as well. Then I wait. While I wait, I make two more calls, leaving messages. Then I wait some more. It's dark now. There's a toenail moon and the ducks on the pond are making a racket, but Arthur is lying quietly. He's not himself. It's either a good sign or a horrible one but since no one is calling me back, I hope for the best. I bring a bucket of water and some hay, which Arthur ignores. So, I scratch his head and wait some more. I hate this part.

Phone silence continued while Arthur reclined in his fluffy manure bed, the Grandfather Horse dozed close by, and I finally retreated, cursing under my breath.

First thing in the morning, I rushed Arthur in to a goat vet. Have I mentioned that Arthur isn't great on a leash? He has two speeds, braced or a dead run, and he flip-flops them without warning. After screeching and stalling our way through four rooms, leaving a trail of bodily fluids and tell-tale droppings, we slam to a stop for x-rays. The broken bones were easy to see. Even from across the room.

This vet used the same nose cone to deliver the anesthesia that they would with a big dog, and once he's knocked out, three of us lift him on the table. Ninety minutes later, Arthur and I are screeching and stalling our way toward the back door of the clinic with a huge cast on his leg. When he sees our horse trailer, he bolts toward it, launching himself in a three-legged broad jump through the air and miraculously lands inside. The vet bill was a little more than twice what I expected, so after I paid it, I took a flying leap into the cab myself, and we headed home.

Arthur had a rough afternoon, but just as he was starting to eat, the vet called and wanted to re-do his cast. At first I said no, but they were afraid that there wasn't enough padding. Neither of us were as well-behaved on the second trip, but a few hours later he was home again, resting in a goat prison with Edgar Rice Burro.

I'd like to gloat an "*I told you so!*" to that goat, wantonly sleeping around without care for hooves or hearts like he did. But I'm just six months out of a cast myself. Okay, it was a Velcro boot, but close enough to recognize that limp. He can barely peg-leg it along; he's lost strength just like I did. He picks up the cast to scratch his ear and it's too heavy, so he sets it down with his head still tilted sideways. An unrequited itch.

The Dude Rancher asked if I thought Arthur would be more

careful in the future. The way he jumped up to limp after the Grandfather Horse before the hoof-print on his leg faded, I can't imagine he will. Truth is we've all got some pretty bad habits around here, but at least none of us are quitters.

BEYOND THE FENCE LINE

I have a neighbor a couple of properties to the north, who brings his cattle home to calve each spring. The pasture is empty the rest of the year but then in one day, twenty-five head materialize, casually grazing. They're hard to miss. The prairie grass is still a monochromatic tan color in all directions and his cattle are Angus—as black as those steel silhouette cutouts of howling coyotes or leaning cowboys. The contrast is dramatic. So is Clara.

My mare stands at the fence line hour after hour, simultaneously attracted and repelled. It's her commitment that alarms me. She loses a fair amount of weight. Apparently, it's hard to eat with them lurking. This is the eighth year she's held her position.

The job gets significantly more difficult about April. By then the calves are on the ground frolicking around like little pepper explosions. Sometimes the cows stroll off toward the rise and the calves dawdle long enough to scare themselves into a tiny stampede to catch up. Surely you can see Clara's problem.

(Maybe some animals have species pride, or are born into predestined gangs, or just have karma to work out. Like dogs and cats. Like horses and cattle.)

In the early years, she could convince our entire equine herd to be concerned and form a line beside her. There was even one Saturday a few years back where all the horses in the group lesson out in the arena participated in some sort of contagious spooking incident, even though they had no idea why. She's like

286

that grade-school boy in the library peering up at the ceiling. I fell for it too many times, only to hear the taunt, "Made you look!"

The old joke isn't funny to Clara; her childhood anxiety is real. I don't know if she loves them or hates them, but she still sounds the alarm; a loud, sharp snort as she stretches a few inches taller. Her tail begins to float up and this time her snort trembles through her whole body. She's universally ignored by the herd as she lifts the front half of her body up into the air and takes a circle so elegant and so sweet, that her hooves barely touch the ground. In the split-second hang time of each stride, her ears point to the intruders. And their horrible, unruly children.

At the late-night walk-through, she's still facing away, standing guard. She looks thin in moonlight so I try to coax her back to the barn to eat her hay with an added flake of alfalfa. The only thing worse than fear is feeling punished for it, so after a few moments, I carry her meal to her work station on the fence line and give her a scratch.

Now her worry has become mine as well. It's contagious. Fear is the most diabolical villain because we hold it close inside of us. From that vantage point, rational thought makes no difference at all.

It occurs to me that I finally understand why people bully fearful horses. It's a defense. A line of demarcation to separate ourselves from the frightened one. Bullies are ironically afraid of being seen as afraid. It would be laughable if it didn't do damage. At the same time, it's probably why fear is such a worthy adversary.

Right about here you want to tell me to give that mare a chance to work stock; that chasing cows will make it all okay. And I hear you. I wasn't born in a dressage saddle, you know.

But there's time. You see, I'm just like Clara; I think too much. Sometimes I get worried about things beyond my fence line, too. All the common sense and rational thought in the world doesn't break my stare. Fear, or the act of denying fear, are equally exhausting. Days like this, we could use a truce for the sake of our hearts. We'd do better to take time to rest awhile with our uncomfortable notions, and find some peace within the boundaries of our little lives.

After all, we don't have to chase every silly cow we see.

WHAT I DIDN'T KNOW THEN

It seems that most things I learn about horses, I learn in hind-sight. It's not a bad thing. Horses learn that way, too.

When I was younger I had a great grasp of the *little picture*. And by that, I mean the same way Wile E. Coyote had a fist around the Roadrunner's long skinny throat…tight enough for reality to have a blackout—his own. I'm not saying I was no fun, but I also believed that patience was an excuse for procrastination. Type A people seemed lazy to me. Clearly it was going to take a horse to get my attention. In a moment of divine intervention, an Appaloosa crossed my path—a weanling, naturally. It was the perfect situation. If you're not averse to changing everything about your life.

I have a shoe-box theory of life. The short version is that the universe has perfect order and reason and love. Sometimes it doesn't look that way because I live in a shoe-box and I can't see over the top. If I was taller, I'd understand, but as it is, I can just do the best I can. Oh, and my shoe-box has a barn in it.

The biggest thing that escaped my limited view, is that there's always a continuum of change: there's the horse you started with, the horse you have now, and the horse he eventually became. Change is a constant but for all the changes that come to pass, the largest changes won't involve your horse at all.

"For a seed to achieve its greatest expression, it must come completely undone. The shell cracks, its insides come out and everything changes. To someone who doesn't understand growth,

it would look like complete destruction." — Cynthia Occelli

When is the best time to start a young horse? The disagreement starts early; studies say that growth plates don't convert to bone for several years. Now some conservatives say wait to start a horse until they're as old as six. It could feel like a waste for an impatient human but horses don't believe in wasted time. Or time at all. On the other hand, the racing industry runs two-year-olds hard. And to spread the blame evenly, a few years ago at a nutrition seminar, most of the questions asked were about how to get Quarter Horses ready to go as long yearlings. Horses live short lives and so we hurry.

In the beginning my young gelding had many huge issues, and by that, I mean me. I had many huge shortcomings that I was very committed to. I'm not proud to say he paid for some of that—not that I blamed him. I blamed everything else instead. That's how he knew I was a keeper.

So, I waited forever and started him at three. In hindsight, I wish I'd given him another year. It's what I've done with every horse since him. With a little more mental maturity some of the issues can be avoided entirely.

Years flew by and we hardly noticed. Then his tendon injury gave me time to question my chosen discipline; lots of reining horses retired early. It was the first time I heard the clock ticking, so I took the leap to dressage. In those days, competition dressage horses were elders, by comparison. That has changed some in the last twenty years, to the shame of contemporary dressage. Practiced properly, dressage can make a horse stronger and buy you more time in the saddle. That was my new goal.

At the same time, I was learning the art of consistency; to quietly ask for his best every day. It wasn't hard for him. By then we were partners and our bickering was replaced by high-level negotiations. But it required more diplomacy and mental focus than I possessed. And physical control was a huge issue; my body, not his.

Is there anything more beautiful than a horse in his prime

with a rider who has figured out how to get out of his way? It feels like a shaft of golden light follows the two of you for every stride. The line between horse and rider gets blurred and if you find a breath of focus so light and open, there are moments when it's impossible to tell where the horse stops and the human starts. Oneness is a shabby, flat word for moments like those.

There's this sweet spot that we call a horse's prime. It's when they are at the height of their physical strength and mental ability; the intersection of fully developed muscles and confident minds, and if a rider happens upon this precious moment with an open heart, magic happens, but it's elation combined with dread. It's why we see professional riders always looking for new horses, even as they ride world-class horses. The work doesn't necessarily destroy them but everyone knows the clock is ticking; that sweet spot is temporary. It isn't going to last longer than any other flower of a moment.

Blink and it's over. Most horses start a slow decline but my gelding had an injury as definite as the flip of a light switch. I've been lucky, my Grandfather Horse survived, and now we've had as many retired years as we had riding years. It's given me extra time for hindsight learning, and the horses who have come after him have all benefited. We owe him a debt, but it's still bittersweet.

Even now we want them to live longer.

It's unkind to force the work past that sweet spot and unkind to force the work before its time. The sad truth about my Grandfather Horse, now thirty, is that his physical prime was truly the shortest time of his life. There was no need to hurry to get there.

In early years, blame was an issue... I reveled in it; horses aren't nearly as attracted to it as humans are. With my usual shoe-box hindsight, I had to acknowledge that our years of connection didn't start when we got it right. My loud thoughts had made a racket inside his head from the beginning. We shared that shoe-box, so of course my horse felt those dark feelings. I had to give up blame entirely. With all that extra room, forgiveness could stretch out and brighten the place up.

If I had it to do over again, I'd start him on day one by forgiving him for having a shorter life. Those were the good old days already.

MANSPLAINING IN THE BARN

Thirty-five years ago, I stood with a group of women protesting a murder sentence given by a judge in Denver. The defendant had shot his estranged wife in the face, point-blank. The judge gave a ridiculously light sentence, saying she had provoked her husband by leaving their marriage. Then in this week's news, reports of a judge gave a puny sentence to a Stanford swimmer, found guilty by jury, of three sexual assault felony convictions. Even after an extremely eloquent statement from the victim. Sometimes it feels like we've made very little progress indeed.

Why would someone who writes about horses speak up on this issue?

Partly because after I was raped, I didn't tell the police or anyone else. When my rapist finished, he mansplained, in a paternal, sarcastic tone, that no one would ever believe me. I crumpled into silence. Well, I got my voice back.

And secondly, because when news about sexual violence hits, we're each sadly reminded of our own pasts, or of those we know who've been hurt, or we have a backward flutter of relief that it wasn't us. Even if the intimidation doesn't rise to the level of violence, when there's a verbal assault or insinuation, the threat still hangs in the air and we can't trust that line between talk and action.

So, what do we do when our hearts hurt, when we need peace, and a friend to lean on? We go to the barn. Some of us have escaped to the barn all our lives.

But there's mansplaining in the barn, too. If you choose a positive training method, you've heard it.

Mansplain means "to explain something to someone, typically a man to woman, in a manner regarded as condescending or patronizing." Lily Rothman of *The Atlantic* defines it as "explaining without regard to the fact that the explainee knows more than the explainer, often done by a man to a woman."

Mansplaining is generally served up with a dose of White Male Privilege. I got in trouble for using that term this week, so if you feel any better, use the traditional term: The Good Old Boys Club. Either way, it's that person who believes in entitlement, likes to be in charge, and can only feel good by putting someone else down. It's the leader who dominates with fear, as if showing disrespect to others is a sign of strength. Be clear: Both men and women mansplain. I just find this term more light hearted than the word we commonly use for women who bully.

Some examples:

The cowboy farrier who told my client (behind my back) I was babying her horse and all any horse needed was a cowboy to ride him. Or the rancher who looked at his twelve-year-old mare, crippled beyond painful imagination, and proudly proclaimed, "We use 'em hard." Or the sheriff's deputy who repeated again and again, to a long-time horse-woman, that horses don't need water; they can live on snow. Or the old cowboy at my book talk who told me that his horses weren't like mine; his horses had to work.

Or the thing I hate the most: A "natural horsemanship" video trainer, who holds a wild-eyed horse's lead-rope short enough to be able to attack the horse's face with his celebrity-whip. All the while he's crashing on the horse, he's playing to the audience and verbally disrespecting the woman who owns the horse—it's always a woman—in the same way that he is disrespecting her horse. She nervously agrees, sharing her horse's fear and confusion.

I don't feel the cowboy magic.

I am sick of seeing spur rowels and steel tie-downs on terrified horses. Tired of horses being shown who's boss, by riders whose insecurity masquerades as bravado. Dominating bullies are so ingrained in our culture, so common, that sometimes we get contrite just to stop the mansplaining short of a bigger fight. We've been taught to hide ourselves in plain sight, in a cloak of silence.

To be clear: I have nothing against cowboys. For crying out loud, Ray Hunt was a cowboy. What I hate is a bully.

And it turns out that the FBI does, too, moving animal cruelty up to a Class A felony, the same as murder and arson. It isn't that the FBI has gone soft for kittens. Statistics show a majority of violent crime begins with animal abuse. If they see cruelty as a precursor to worse violence, shouldn't we?

The second reason I know this is a big deal, is the number of emails and comments I get from riders who resist being told by trainers that fear equals respect, and that we must have our horse's respect at all costs. They're relieved to find training methods that value intuition over violence; thrilled to experience an even better response from a horse for NOT being a bully. They understand that a horse can clearly tell the difference between kindness and weakness.

Thoughtful horse-people know that rodeo isn't the highest form of horsemanship. They train with gentle hands, take good care of their horses, and show respect for others. Having compassion can sometimes be as challenging as riding a bull, but they lift the conversation above name-calling and innuendo, and stand up for others, patiently holding space for them until they can stand up for themselves.

A special reminder to horse-women; we *ARE* the horse world. We're literally 80 percent of the competitors at shows, and the percentage of pleasure riders is probably larger. At the Olympics and other world competitions, women compete—not in "ladies" classes—but as equals to men. And we frequently win. Women are a huge financial power; we outspend men by far. Instead of that being a joke, *we* should take it seriously. Money is power.

And perhaps the most world-changing women's trait; we understand, usually first hand, that fear and domination do not equal good leadership. We know that just like intimidating women and kids doesn't create a trusting relationship, neither will harsh training techniques create a committed equine partner. Fear will never be a dependable motivator as long as the victim has a heart beating and a breath to move forward.

Horses teach us to elevate the conversation; that a small, well-timed *ask-and-reward* is always kinder and more effective that a huge fight.

So, the next time you find yourself standing in a puddle of mansplaining, take a breath. Put a smile on your face and speak the truth: "Deputy, that just isn't right." Or take your horse's reins back from the rider who wants to "help" by teaching your horse a lesson with these words: "No thanks, I'll take it from here." Stand up to bullies and hold your ground with your own calm, but equally proud proclamation: "We don't do it that way here."

IF WISHES WERE HORSES

"How much does a horse cost? Do you have to be rich to own one?"

I can tell you how much hay they eat, warn you about vet bills and farrier visits. There are many articles and books written about equine economics, but the first truth anyone learns is that owning a horse is nowhere near that easy to quantify.

I know talking about money is rude, or at least uncomfortable. Still, I'm endlessly curious. Money is a vehicle that carries dreams and wishes into the real world; simple math done on a spiritual obstacle course.

Lottery winners and philosophers tell us that money doesn't buy happiness. Words that are foolish and flat when compared to the vast return we get from a puppy's adoption fee. Or your first horse. Money has a concrete value but we always must reconcile that literal value with our personal feeling of abundance or lack.

Let's begin here: If we were somehow required to have a bank account to cover any issues that might come up in the future in the lives of our animal companions, most of us could barely afford one cat. So, this is where the magic comes in. It isn't obvious divine intervention; hay bales don't multiply in a loaves-and-fishes miracle. Sometimes it's barely noticeable, like the truck *doesn't* break down or a few months go by *without* emergency vet calls.

Just when you get comfortable, money goes worthless. It can

purchase a horse, but it's never been able to buy relationship and skill in the saddle. Horses are the great equalizer; you can't buy the ride. Or the other priceless things: freedom, friendship, and self-esteem.

If money is a vehicle, it's still up to us to steer it. One horse-woman complains bitterly about the cost of her farrier and always asks for a discount. She also drives a brand-new red sports car; I notice the tires are good. I met a man who admitted that he'd spent $40,000 on surgery for his dog's brain injury. He was so sad about losing the dog, but not the money. Some of us have brand new trucks and skinny horses. Some of us need a larger geriatric pen, while others switch horses in and out every year without a second thought. It's investment and return. Are you horse rich or horse poor?

In my case, I knew the costs early. I'd paid for my horse with babysitting money as a kid. After I left home, I was responsible. I waited, counting every dollar and every miserable day, until I was... well, *stable*. I knew the costs of keeping a horse as well as the costs of living without one. I had a plan and a budget. And six months after bringing my new horse home, my husband filed for divorce. Surprise, I didn't have that in the budget.

It can all feel like chaos. Do your very best, yet all the plans, prayers, and affirmations won't hold if the universe has a different lesson in mind. The only thing you can count on is that money will be an ingredient in that kind of disaster every time. Then, against the odds, the truest blessings in life come right after the very worst days. Depend on that like money in the bank, too.

When I look around my circle of friends, not everyone is where they thought they would be financially. Okay, nobody is. Life happens and everything changes in a blink. Health issues develop, work changes, relationships crash, and we've already re-invented ourselves more than once. Life throws us a few curve-balls but even then, past the whining and bragging and wishing, it's easy to know a person's true priority. It's as clear as a check register. We put our money where our heart is.

How do I budget? Sometimes I must make hard decisions. I always know that I can't afford catastrophic surgery. Spending several thousand dollars on one animal isn't possible if it endangers the well-being of the whole herd. I've been lucky with that side; the universe knows my budget and doesn't push me too hard. I've learned to trust that.

I think the first thing I ever charged was a vet bill and I'm usually paying off one animal bill or another. At this point, it's nostalgic. Beyond that, we all agree it's about quality of life and that's what we celebrate here. There are always a few seniors who are frail. It isn't a crime to get old and when it's time, I'm happy to ease their way. Financial debt has become part of the mourning process. Everything heals in time, money and hearts.

Keeping horses gets more expensive each year and the days of a rural culture with horses grazing in the pasture are fading. I'd hate it if horses became a hobby only for the wealthy and I fear lives in the middle, like mine, will become even more challenging. If the day comes that horses aren't around to save horse-crazy little girls and give them wings, it would be a very sad time. So, I'll hold to this little farm and pay my blessings forward.

Am I on the road to becoming that crazy cat lady, only different? A crazy horse-woman with a full barn and gnarled hands perpetually gripping a muck fork? I hope so. I can't put a dollar value on the particular smell of a horse's mane, or the warmth of a donkey pressing his head to my back, or the sound of dog paws following along. In the end, it's easy to live the dream. You just give up everything else.

But money remains a mystery to me. I know it's somehow attached to the Circle of Life because I've seen the two of them whispering together. If money is a vehicle, then as far as I can tell, I've always had outside help turning the wheel.

"How much does a horse cost?" I'd say they cost everything you have.

"Do you have to be rich to own one?" No, that comes later.

THE FINE ART OF CANTANKERY

I've always had a hard time acting my age. That's not it, exactly. It's more like I'm straddling the Grand Canyon between my ongoing teen angst and dealing with the fact I'm supposed to be wearing support hose. It all started with my birthday—the big one I had two years ago.

Then recently a donkey was relinquished to the horse rescue that I work with. She was nothing special, really. Her "selling point" was her age, I guess. We joked about needing to carbon date her. We're guessing upper thirties. At least. Her neck has broken over into a slouch and there's a hitch in her hind. She has no teeth and a few seasons of hair, felted into a crusty shell over her body. She's squeamish about people, but that's just sound common sense.

It had been her job to protect calves from coyote, but the cattle left the land a decade ago. It was just her and a lame gelding, with no way to run. Did she stand her ground and bray when the coyotes came? Her voice is still strong. She's prairie tough but being "rescued" nearly killed her.

Rule #1: Donkeys hate change.

She arrived at our rescue facility and landed in a peaceful geriatric pen with other special-needs cases. Nobody was too active and there was a buffet; piles of hay, lots of fresh water, and feed pans brimming with senior feed. In short, paradise. But she was having none of it. She had more opinion than strength.

***

Where am I? Where'd you take my horse-friend? I've been kid-napped!

***

There's an argument that she'd already had a long life. On top of that, the rescue had just gotten fourteen head of starved year-lings in that needed foster homes. For me, there's no rhyme or reason why one particular animal catches my eye in this world of need; I usually learn in hindsight. So, I offered to take this old girl to my barn. It's slower and quieter here, and she was pretty wobbly. If taking on an antique donkey when so many young horses need help sounds counter-intuitive, well, it has something to do with being of an age where you get told to wear those stupid support hose.

Coming to my farm was not a miracle cure. She still didn't eat or drink anything. Donkeys are tough, but what if it was too late and her organs were shutting down?

***

Leave me alone. I hate everything.

***

She played with alfalfa but ignored hay. A few times a day, I tried some new mush concoction but she was not impressed. Donkeys are notoriously nervous about water containers. If she was drinking, I couldn't tell, so I tried changing those as well. On the third day, I used an old blue bucket and finally, she drank.

***

Just a sip.

***

Rule #2: Donkeys please themselves.

In the meantime, I sat in her pen, just sharing space. I already knew she wasn't wild about being caught or led. She came with a warning that she didn't like her ears being touched. Or apparently, anything else for that matter.

Then one day I was in her pen cutting up an over-ripe pear to put on her mush, which was already the equine equivalent of a fine French meal. This pear was sticky-sweet and soft, and she inched her way to me. Her sense of smell was perfect. It took a long while, I sat very still, but she took a bite of the pear from my hand. Her face went soft and I could hear it sloshing around in her mouth. I dropped the rest of the pear onto her mush and left the pen. Of course, standing up meant that she backed off from her bowl for a moment, but I wanted to be mysterious and exciting.

People get too hung up on rescue animals' histories. We love a tragic tale so we can feel sympathy and "*tsk-tsk*" and shake our do-gooder heads. If there's one thing I know about rescue, it's that the past doesn't matter nearly like the present does. Says the post-hormonal woman who wears her teen angst around her ankles like stretched out cotton underwear.

Rule #3: Donkeys can be, well, cantankerous.

She tolerates grooming but just to the middle of her flank. I still haven't picked up a foot. But the flies were eating her legs raw and I needed to get some ointment on her wounds. She gave me a solid *NO*, but I was marginally successful despite her efforts and she was steaming mad about it. Then I gingerly tried fly spray. She darted but then paused. I sprayed again. There were enough flies still there that I could see them drop off her leg and hit the ground. It's possible she saw them, too. Now when I walk to her with the fly spray, she stands and waits, as if I'm serving boat drinks at the beach. Clearly no signs of dementia.

***

It doesn't mean I'm happy about it.

***

I started to think she might pull through; I started to think her name might be Lilith. Just on the off-chance that you're *cooing* and thinking she is just the sweetest thing… she isn't. She bites. And kicks. She almost tolerates grooming, but a hand anywhere near her poll and she tosses her head abruptly. Like me, she's still touchy about her feet…and she can kick as high as my knee now. She's a donkey of strong convictions.

She was staying in a quiet pen with Arthur, the goat, who was still in detention with a broken leg. They formed a bond of codependent aggravation. Sometimes Arthur tried to steal her lunch. She'd pull her floppy lips up high and open her jaw to an outlandishly wide angle and threaten the goat, eventually leaving a massive wet spot on the goat's shoulder. Decrepit intimidation.

***

Back-off, Whippersnapper. I'll eat your ear.

***

On a day that I could catch her, I doddered her out to the greenest grass for a different kind of dental exam. She dropped her head and slowly rubbed her nose back and forth, crushing it and sniffing deeply. She didn't even try to take a bite. Her lips can scoop up mush, but her front teeth are useless. You know those billboards that show drug addicts with horrible teeth? That's her. She has greenish-black nubbins of teeth. Meth teeth, so no worries about eating any goats.

Cantankerous defined: 1. bad-tempered, argumentative, uncooperative, quarrelsome; irascible, disagreeable. 2. Difficult to handle.

Eventually Lilith stopped standing outside during thunderstorms and went into the shed. Once she crossed that line, she used the shed for shade, too. One day she went to the gate to my family pen and turned her head to stare at me. I pride myself on being bilingual, so I opened the gate for her.

***

They'll probably be horrible.

***

That pen had the Grandfather Horse, Edgar Rice Burro, and the rest of my herd. Five minutes of careful consideration later, she took a step through the gate. The mares push her off sometimes, but she kicks back at them. She can get her hind end a few inches off the ground these days. Lilith takes long naps in the sun and tries to get someone to do some mutual grooming. The Grandfather Horse, who's always loved the stiffest curry, finds her an unsatisfactory partner. It's mutual gumming, to tell the truth.

***

Grandfather? You aren't near as old as me. Do that some more.

***

Rule #4: Donkeys don't like change, unless they do.

So now this ancient donkey thinks my ratty little farm is the most elite equine facility in the world. Perception really is all that matters.

It's been four months since Lilith came. She's sleek, she has lousy ground manners, and she's in fine voice. Her bray sounds like a combination of a train whistle and a bunch of sixth-grade boys making fart noises. And she isn't afraid to use it.

***

Woman, come stand with us. I like your touch. I'll kick you if you get near my feet.

***

Right now, we're debating the last feed of the day. She holds, loudly, that I should always feed at sundown. With the season change, I tell her the sun sets earlier. I tell her it was always about the time on the clock. Then she makes it pretty clear what she thinks about clocks.

***

Hey, you! We're hungry out here.

***

Measuring time is a peculiarity to our species. Clocks and calendars rule humans. I miss my friends who've timed-out and retired to warm climates. Meanwhile I throw hay and think about reinventing myself one more time. I'm stubborn about what I want and I'm at an awkward age.

On the high side, I've finally found my spirit animal.

Anna Blake was born in Cavalier County, North Dakota, in 1954, the youngest daughter of a farm family. Currently she's a horse advocate, award-winning author, and equine pro, living on the Colorado prairie. Infinity Farm is home to a multi-species herd of horses, llamas, goats, and everyone's moral compass, Edgar Rice Burro.

OTHER BOOKS BY ANNA BLAKE:

Stable Relation: A Memoir of One Woman's Spirited Journey Home, by Way of the Barn

When most women go through a mid-life crisis, they start a diet, get plastic surgery, or have an affair. My life went to the dogs…and horses…and llamas… and did I mention happy hour with the goats? It's the memoir of a bittersweet transition from a mid-life orphan to a modern pioneer woman, building an entirely different kind of family farm.

Relaxed & Forward: Relationship Advice from Your Horse

Humans have been besotted with horses since they had three toes. From the popular Relaxed and Forward blog comes training advice written in brief "daily devotionals" combining the everyday fundamentals of dressage with mutual listening skills. Written with a profound respect for horses and an articulate voice, blending equal parts humor, inspiration, and un-common sense.

79729049R10176

Made in the USA
Columbia, SC
29 October 2017